STUDIES IN SAMARITAN MANUSCRIPTS AND ARTIFACTS

AMERICAN SCHOOLS OF ORIENTAL RESEARCH
MONOGRAPH SERIES

edited by
David Noel Freedman

Number 1

STUDIES IN SAMARITAN MANUSCRIPTS AND ARTIFACTS
THE CHAMBERLAIN-WARREN COLLECTION

by
Robert T. Anderson

STUDIES IN SAMARITAN MANUSCRIPTS AND ARTIFACTS
THE CHAMBERLAIN-WARREN COLLECTION

by

Robert T. Anderson

Published by

THE AMERICAN SCHOOLS OF ORIENTAL RESEARCH

Distributed by

THE AMERICAN SCHOOLS OF ORIENTAL RESEARCH
126 Inman Street
Cambridge, MA 02139

STUDIES IN SAMARITAN MANUSCRIPTS AND ARTIFACTS
THE CHAMBERLAIN-WARREN COLLECTION

by

Robert T. Anderson

Library of Congress Cataloging in Publication Data

Anderson, Robert T   1928-
    Studies in Samaritan manuscripts and artifacts — the
Chamberlain-Warren collection.

    (Monograph Series - American Schools of Oriental
Research ; no. 1)
    Bibliography: p.
    1. Manuscripts, Samaritan — Michigan — East
Lansing — Catalogs. 2. Chamberlain, Frederic W. —
Library — Catalogs. 3. Warren, Edward K., 1847-1919—
Library — Catalogs. I. Title. II. Series: American
Schools of Oriental Research. Monograph Series -
American Schools of Oriental Research ; no. 1.
Z6621.M6122X483   016.091   78-52697

ISBN 0-89757-401-X

Printed in the United States of America

PREFACE

In general, I have tried to model this study after the Catalogue of the Samaritan Manuscripts in the John Rylands Library. However, there remained the difficulties of consistently transliterating Semitic names and other words, the limitations imposed by personal language competencies, and compromises that often seemed wise in the stating of statistics. I have tried to be consistent in the way Semitic words are spelled, but alternative spellings in quotations and the use of the same names in both Arabic and Samaritan language contexts have called for some arbitrary decisions. I have not used critical marks in names on the assumption that anyone who understood the marks would be thoroughly familiar with the names. Given my particular limitations with Arabic, I have not tried to transliterate the Arabic text, since I could not comment meaningfully upon it. Indications of numbers of lines per page or letters per line in manuscripts are averages based on sample counts at various points in the text.

The designation "two letter" or "one letter" is used in referring to types of manuscripts. The terms refer to the number of letters used by the scribe to line up the left margin of a column. In the older manuscripts, one letter would be set at the left margin and a large gap often exists between it and the penultimate letter. Later, two letters were used for the same purpose.

More detail on the three oldest manuscripts in the collection, particularly the location of lacunae in the text, is contained in three articles in the *Revue biblique* written by the author (Anderson 1970: 68-75; 1970a: 550-60; 1972: 368-80).

TABLE OF CONTENTS

Page

PREFACE v

LIST OF FIGURES ix

INTRODUCTION 1

    Nablus to East Lansing 1

    The Samaritans 4

    Religious Beliefs and Practices 5

    Characteristics of the Written Language 6

    Significance of Samaritan Studies 8

THE PENTATEUCHS 9

    The Samaritan Pentateuch 9

    CW 2473 11

    CW 2478a 15

    CW 2478b 22

    CW 2484 23

    CW 2481 31

    CW 2482 38

    CW 2483 42

    CW 10311 43

    CW 10262 44

    CW 2467, 10316, 10317, 10318, 10322 47

    CW 11704 47

    CW 2468 47

    CW 10320 (20 Volumes), 10309, 10314, and Two Other Volumes 48

THE INSCRIPTIONS 59

    The Marble Inscription: CW 2472 59

    CW 2472 59

    The Brass Scroll Case: CW 2465 62

MARKAH 65

    Markah: CW 26349 65

LITURGICAL TEXTS 69

    Samaritan Liturgies 69

    CW 2480 70

    CW 2486 73

    CW 10312 75

    CW 10313 77

    CW 26343 78

    CW 26344 79

FIGURES 83

BIBLIOGRAPHY 95

LIST OF FIGURES

1. CW 2473, Gen 19:20-38.

2. CW 2473, Lev 22:9-22:27.

3. CW 2473, end of Leviticus.

4. CW 2478, end of Genesis.

5. CW 2478, end of Exodus.

6. CW 2478b, The Exodus Fragment; Exod 25:39-26:4.

7. CW 2478b, The Exodus Fragment; Exod 25:27-32.

8. CW 2472, The Marble Inscription.

9. CW 2484, end of Genesis.

10. CW 2484, Exod 20:7-end of decalogue plus a Samaritan addition.

11. CW 2484, Deut 8:3-16.

12. CW 2478, Deut 6:11-22.

In 1967 an article appeared in the *Revue biblique* describing a series of six Samaritan inscriptions (Strugnell 1967: 555-80). The first inscription, the author noted, was not available to him except in the form of a casting he had located in Jerusalem. A note dated the casting in the last century. He searched for the original, contacting the American Schools of Oriental Research, the American Institute of Archaeology, the Oriental Institute of the University of Chicago, the University Museum at Philadelphia and the Kelsey Museum of Archaeology at Ann Arbor. All denied having it. A few months later their denial was substantiated when the missing inscription appeared in a cardboard box in a storage room under the football stadium at Michigan State University.

The odyssey of the stone from Jerusalem to East Lansing leaves many stages clouded in mystery, but a key link was Mr. E. K. Warren, a wealthy churchman from Three Oaks, MI, who met the Samaritans during a visit to Palestine in 1901. He became very much involved with the community, giving them financial assistance and acquiring from them a number of manuscripts and other artifacts. In 1950 these items along with hundreds of other unrelated items from Warren's collection were given to Michigan State University. The director of the University Museum consulted several universities and museums, sending photographs and descriptions of the marble inscription and 15th century A.D. Pentateuchs with the explicit suggestion that some other university could make better use of them. Only one scholar expressed any interest at all, and the materials were placed in storage under the stadium until they could be cataloged.

That interval turned out to be 18 years. I received a call in the spring of 1968 asking if I would try to evaluate some materials that Mr. Warren had brought from Palestine. With some initial guidance from Professor James Purvis of Boston University and Professor John Strugnell of Harvard I set about surveying the collection. Reading the introduction to August von Gall's *Der Hebräische Pentateuch der Samaritaner* (1914-1918) I came upon a reference to a brass scroll case which, according to the text, had been bought by E. K. Warren. It was soon located in another storage area of the University Museum. A chance conversation with a librarian uncovered several more volumes, including the copy of *Memar Markah*, in the vault of the University Library.

I believe the materials are now all together. In this volume is a description of the contents of the collection and its relationship to other Samaritan materials that are known through catalogs, journals, and other publications. The remainder of this chapter describes the origins of this particular collection with comments on the Samaritan people who produced it.

Nablus to East Lansing

Three years after his first trip to Palestine, Mr. Warren chartered a ship to bring 800 delegates to the World Sunday School Association convention in Jerusalem. Jakob, the high priest of the Samaritan community, addressed the convention and Warren felt that it was "the most striking event of the convention" (Purvis 1972). During the succeeding fifteen years, Warren became increasingly taken with the problems of the Samaritans.

Some of his projects, like the establishment of schools for both boys and girls, were quite practical, but others bordered on fantasy.

At one time he set up a meeting of Samaritans and Jews in Paris with the hope of healing the 2500 year schism between the two groups. Another time he was hopeful that the Samaritans were in possession of ancient documents that would verify the gospel accounts about Jesus.

One of his dreams, a dream that eventually determined the arrival of the present collection in Michigan, had an air of practicality, but never was fulfilled. As a means of helping the community to become financially self sufficient, an American Samaritan Committee was established during the meeting of the World Sunday School Convention at Zurich in 1913 with Mr. Warren as chairman and Professor F. S. Goodrich of Albion College as secretary. The most prominent of the other members was the Reverend William E. Barton, an American clergyman who published several articles on the Samaritans and aided in the editing and publishing of works written by the high priest, Jakob. Mr. Barton also collected some Samaritan writings which he gave to Boston University (Purvis 1972).

Several individuals living in Palestine acted as agents on behalf of the committee. Mr. R. Floyd, a Palestinian travel agent, and Mr. Fareed worked with the Committee in its early period. According to one source, Fareed was the agent in the purchase by Mr. Warren of the brass scroll case CW 2405 (Purvis 1972: 12, n. 8). At some point Mr. John Whiting, United States Vice-Counsel in Jerusalem was designated as the official Palestinian representative of the committee. He arranged for the photographing of the Abischua scroll and was instrumental in the purchase of several Samaritan manuscripts, including 26344 and 10313 of this collection as attested by the colophons. He was unavailable at times because of political intelligence work he was doing with the British army and this, combined with his interpersonal ineptness, finally alienated both the Samaritans and the American committee.

Although there were efforts to solicit money publicly for the support of the Committee most of the funds were supplied by Mr. Warren. To raise more money Warren had encouraged the publication of photographs of the famous Abischua scroll purportedly written by the great grandson of Aaron. He expected a reasonable profit to accrue to the Samaritans from the sale of the photos to museums and universities around the world. The photos were taken but for various reasons, particularly the poor quality of the photos and the judgment of a well-known Old Testament scholar that the manuscript was not authentic, they did not sell.

Meanwhile the Committee was buying such manuscripts as it could find to assure that they would not leave Palestine. They intended that they should be housed eventually in a local museum when funds could be found for its construction. It was assumed that the Samaritans would repurchase their sacred writings and use them to attract a tourist trade that would sustain the community. At the same time Warren was apparently buying other items like the marble inscription and possibly the brass scroll case on his own. Since some of these items remained in Palestine for a long time after their purchase, Warren may have intended that they also be preserved for the day when a museum would be built. The Samaritans in their destitution were selling their possessions pretty freely and it was the concern of the members of the Committee to buy them and keep them within reach of the Samaritans.

In 1919 Mr. Warren died, interest in the museum dwindled, the Samaritans had no fund with which to redeem their manuscripts and most of them were sent to Three Oaks, MI, as part of Warren's estate. Barton wrote in 1921:

The committee owns several manuscripts believed to be ancient and deposited in Palestine awaiting its order, and a larger number of recent manuscripts made by the Samaritans. It is agreed that all personal property, excepting photographic plates, belonging to this Committee, shall be forwarded to this country; that the older manuscripts be deposited for the present in the libraries of prominent universities, where they will have care and be available for Scholarly study; the recent manuscripts to be placed on sale and the proceeds to be deposited in the treasury of the committee for the ultimate benefit of the Samaritan people (Barton 1921: 21).

In fact they were housed in a museum that Warren had started in Three Oaks to display several collections that the family had brought back from various world travels. His son-in-law, F. W. Chamberlain, made the shipping arrangements. From the invoices a picture, often confusing, may be gleaned of the items sent.

The number of items being considered is itself a problem. According to the invoice there could have been seventy items. Since there are only fifty items in the present collection (and this includes several that are not on the invoice) it means that there are at least twenty items missing. Some of these may have been sold or given away by Warren or Chamberlain, or there may be a cache still to be discovered.

A consideration of some of the more important items reveals other problems, particularly with those Mr. Warren bought on his own. According to von Gall and H. Spoer (1906: 105-7) Warren bought the brass scroll case some time prior to 1906, probably during his stay there in 1904. However, according to a note attached to the scroll case by the Three Oaks Museum staff, the scroll case was a gift to Mr. Warren from the High Priest Jakob in December of 1913. Mr. Warren's son claimed that all the materials were gifts, but the Three Oaks notes indicate prices of at least two of the old Pentateuchs ($1,500 for 2478a and $500 for 2484) and Warren describes paying $1,000 for a manuscript for himself (Sunday School Times, July 20, 1918), perhaps CW 2473. The value of the manuscripts is approximated in both letters and invoices without stating that it was the price paid. No figures are mentioned in connection with the brass scroll case or the marble inscription. According to Warren's son the latter was purchased (!) in Nablus in 1901. So we are left with a number of perplexing questions: were the items gifts or purchases? Did the scroll case come into Mr. Warren's hands in 1904 or 1913? Where are the items listed on the invoice that are not in the present collection? Which items were bought by the American Samaritan Committee to be left in Nablus and which items did Mr. Warren purchase for himself? According to Professor Purvis another manuscript which he believes to be CW 2478a was sent to America in 1921 (1972: 12). If so, there is an extra parchment manuscript on the 1920 invoice whose whereabouts is unknown.

At this point, Mr. Warren's dream had dissipated, leaving the Samaritans in rather unfortunate circumstances. They had neither realized profit from the photographs of the Abischua scroll nor succeeded in keeping the manuscripts in Palestine. They communicated with the American Samaritan Committee for two or three years trying to secure more money and/or the return of their manuscripts. Mr. Barton went to Palestine in 1926 and distributed the assets of the Committee and this phase in the history of these

4

manuscripts was closed. For the next quarter of
a century they remained in the Three Oaks Museum.
When the Museum was closed a generation later,
Mr. Fred Warren made arrangements to have the
contents delivered to Michigan State University.

The Samaritans

Although there are very few materials extant
that predate the earliest items in the Chamberlain-Warren collection, the history of the people
that produced them long predates existing artifacts. It would be proper to infer that there is
a great deal of obscurity surrounding the early
history of the Samaritans.

Their roots are in northern Palestine and
much of the animosity between Samaritan and Jew
reflects the continuing animosity between the
highly institutionalized, agriculturally orient-
ed, culture of northern Palestine and the more
nomadic sheepherding culture of the South. Since
the South became the home of normative Judaism
there was a continuing negative critique of the
practices of the north. Abel's animal offering
was preferable to Cain's vegetable offering,
Noah was chastized for drinking the fruit of the
cultivated grape, the Rechabites and Nazirites
exemplified their purity by resisting agriculture
and clinging to a bedouin way of existence. The
Samaritans were clearly from the North and thus,
from the viewpoint of normative Judaism, had the
wrong geography, politics, and history.

No disinterested party was on the scene to
record how Jew and Samaritan became distinct
entities and each tells quite a different tale.
Jewish tradition speaks of the Samaritans as de-
cendents of the various peoples imported into
northern Palestine from such places as Babylon,
Cutha, and Hamath by the Assyrians in conse-
quence of their ascendancy over the area during
the eighth and seventh centuries B.C. The tradition goes on to say that these alien people
were beset by an invasion of lions and in their
desperation asked for a priest of Yahweh to
teach them how to worship properly that they
might be delivered from the lions. This would
explain why the Samaritans share in common the
Torah and the major festivals. It also explains
why the Samaritans have been referred to as "men
of Cutha" and "lion converts" by Jewish writers.

Samaritan tradition speaks otherwise. They
trace Samaritan origins to the northern tribes
of Israel, claiming that the Assyrian deporta-
tion was neither complete nor long lasting. Samaritans see themselves as the conservators of
the original Israelite faith and the Jews as
schismatics who broke away at the time that Eli
set up a sanctuary at Shiloh rather than at Mt.
Gerizim. The E document or northern Mosaic tradition of the Pentateuch is more evident in subsequent Samaritan theology than either J or P
(MacDonald 1963: xli). Their very name, they
say, testifies to their faithfulness in main-
taining the original tradition. The etymology
of their name, by their claim, is "the obser-
vant," rather than "inhabitants of Samaria." A
basic truth lies behind both claims. Whatever
their vicissitudes, the people of the northern
kingdom did not maintain their identity as
clearly during their subjugation to the Assyrians as the people of the southern kingdom did
during their subjugation in Babylon. The issue
was forced during the post-exilic period as
people of the South demonstrated increasing un-
willingness to include the people of the North
in their religious community. But recent studies demonstrate that the issue is more complex
than either tradition reflects (Coggins 1975;
Purvis 1968). Rather than a dramatic schism,
there was more likely a gradual drifting apart
that was not explicitly pronounced until the 2nd
or 1st century B.C.

Roots of the separation lie in the tensions

between north and south and the treatment of the northerners by the Assyrians in the 8th century B.C. Both traditions agree that the alienation was intensified in the latter part of the 5th century B.C. as the Samaritans found themselves in conflict with Nehemiah (according to biblical tradition) or Ezra (according to the Samaritan tradition). The exclusiveness and purity demanded by Ezra may have been particularly instrumental in the evolution of heterodox labels for the Samaritans.

The cleavage was on its way to finality when the Samaritans rebelled against Alexander the Great (Wright 1971: 4). In return Alexander destroyed Samaria and settled 600 troops there. The Samaritans fled to Mt. Gerizim and with the permission of Alexander built a temple very similar to the Jerusalem temple (Campbell 1969: 7). John Hyracanus, a Jewish governor and high priest added a final depth of animosity to the schism when he destroyed Shechem and ravaged the Samaritan temple about 128 B.C. Once the Jews lost political control of all of Palestine to the Romans, the fate of Jews and Samaritans was joined and they suffered persecution or oppression together at the hands of the Romans.

Sometime in the early Christian era there was a flowering of Samaritan theology, epitomized in the work of Markah, who apparently lived in the fourth century A.D. Remnants of Samaritan synagogues suggest reasonable prosperity until the time of the emperor Justinian. At that time, in A.D. 529, the Samaritans tried unsuccessfully to rebel and were suppressed with such severity that they never really recovered. In 636 they fell to Muslim rule, in 1099 the crusaders entered and in 1244 the Muslims returned.

During these periods of oppression the Samaritans, like the Jew, often fled and colonies of Samaritans appeared in various places throughout the Mediterranean world. There was a synagogue in Thessalonica and by the end of the sixth century, one also in Rome. Tyre, Caesarea, Ascalon, Gaza and particularly Damascus and Cairo became centers of the Samaritan *diaspora* in the Middle East.

In recent centuries the Samaritans have continued to survive, but only with great hardship. During the nineteenth century they were denied access to their sacred mountain. Their literary efforts have long since dwindled. Their numbers are down to a few hundred. Many of them have moved from Nablus to other parts of Israel, particularly Holon near Tel Aviv.

European interest in the Samaritans was triggered originally in 1616 when Pietro della Valle brought back to Europe a Pentateuch and other writings. In the late nineteenth century other European scholars spearheaded a revival of interest in the community and manuscripts of their literature were acquired in increasing quantity. There are now extensive holdings in this field in the British Museum, the Bodleian, the Vatican, the Hebrew University, the John Rylands Library and the Hermitage in Leningrad.

Religious Beliefs and Practices

The Samaritan creed succinctly outlines the basic beliefs: "We say: My faith is in thee, YHWH; and in Moses son of Amram, thy servant, and in the Holy Law; and in Mount Gerizim Bethel; and in the Day of Vengeance and Recompense" (Montgomery 1968: 207).

An absolute monotheism is central to the Samaritan faith; it is a monotheism paralleling the rigorous affirmation of Islam. The statement of both these faiths may reflect a reaction to the trinitarian formulation of Christianity. God is most commonly referred to as El or Ela (akin to the Islamic Allah) but the tetragrammaton is also in regular use. Samaritans avoid

6

the use of images more than the Jews, but they
show less anxiety about the divine name, a pro-
nunciation of which still survives. God has revealed himself through the Creation and the
Torah.

The Torah is a second basic affirmation of
the Samaritan community. It is God's law and almost always accompanied by the adjective "holy."
It is copied carefully by hand on parchment or
good paper. It is read at all religious services. Wealthy families own beautifully printed
copies which are passed down through many generations. The central cultural artifact of the Samaritan community is the Torah said to have been
copied by Abischua, grandson of Aaron, which is
housed in the modest synagogue at Nablus and
proudly displayed to tourists. Once a year it is
displayed for the special adoration of the congregation.

Moses is the mediator between God and man in
the reception of the Law and his adoration con-
stitutes a third focus of Samaritan faith. He is
the last of the prophets and the most exalted.
Many blessings are in the name of Moses the
faithful. Parallels between Samaritan adoration
of Moses and Christian adoration of Jesus are
close and perhaps intentional (MacDonald 1964:
ch. 22).

Mount Gerizim is uniquely connected with
God. In Samaritan tradition, it is the navel of
the world. There Abel built the first altar and
there Abraham was willing to sacrifice Isaac. It
is the highest mountain in the world and its peak
survived the flood. A special insertion after
the decalogue in the Samaritan Pentateuch under-
scores Gerizim as God's holy mountain. Upon
Gerizim the Samaritans still hold their chief
festivals.

To these major features, it is customary to
add a fifth tenet, though it is by no means as
visible in the materials of the Chamberlain-
Warren collection or any other general collec-

tion. A random colophon would very likely refer
to God, the Torah and Moses; it might include a
reference to Mount Gerizim. The mention of es-
chatology to say nothing of its discussion is
pretty much limited to the *Memar Markah*, the
basic theological work of the Samaritans. There
it is implied that the end of religion is attain-
ment of the Day of Reward when the faithful are
led to the garden of Eden.

Circumcision and celebration of the Sabbath
are the common rituals of the Samaritans. Sabbath is strictly observed with services in the
synagogue. The main festival of the synagogue
is the Day of Atonement when the Law is read and
the Abischua Scroll is exhibited for adoration.

The remaining services are held on Mount
Gerizim. This includes Passover, the coincidental but distinct Festival of Unleavened Bread
and Pentacost, celebrated the 50th day after the
first Passover Sabbath. Passover is the holiest
of Samaritan festivals and during its course,
lambs are sacrificed, the last vestige of explicit animal sacrifice among the religions of the
West.

Characteristics of the Written Language

Like the Jews, the Samaritans expressed
themselves basically in literary rather than pic-
torial or plastic media. Their scripture was
the Pentateuch and they retained an intentionally archaic form of writing as they passed it
down through the centuries. Accordingly, Samaritan writing in the 20th century still uses Hebrew characters akin to those of the 2nd century
B.C. Because of this practiced archaism and the
paucity of artifacts, the dating of inscriptions
has been particularly difficult.

Like other Semitic languages, Samaritan Hebrew is written from right to left. The letters
are hung from a top line which is often incised

into the parchment or stone before the script begins. Inscriptions and Pentateuchs are usually in majuscle letters written with considerable care. Liturgical texts and various treaties are usually done in a cursive hand that ranges from quite neat to practical illegibility.

Both liturgical and biblical texts have a variety of ornamentation. The conclusion of a part of a manuscript, for example the end of one of the biblical books or the liturgy for a particular service, often provides the occasion for some artistic embellishment. At minimum this consists of some pattern repeated horizontally across the page to separate the end of the text from any further annotation. C and V shaped marks, zigzag lines and dots are commonly used. Short blessings or comments on dates and authorship may have boxes drawn around them in similar patterns. Within the text several means of decoration are used. In liturgical texts it is fairly common for several biblical verses to be arranged in triangular shapes of alternating colors. Purple ink is the most common alternative to black, but green and red are also used.

In their liturgies, the Samaritans have been fond of acrostic poems in which the lines begin with successive letters of the alphabet. A different type of acrostic (tashqil) is used in texts of the Pentateuch. The scribe leaves a channel vertically through the center of the text and, as he writes the text, he drops into the channel those letters which when read from top to bottom convey his message. He may give information about himself or indicate the middle of the Torah or insert some blessing or slogan. A last means of decorating the manuscripts is the alignment of vertical columns of letter and words. When possible the scribe of a Pentateuch watches for a place where the same letter or word occurs in subsequent lines at approximately the same place and then intentionally shifts the lines so that the letter or words will form a

column. This often necessitates having considerable blank space on one side or another of the column. The column may extend from two to more than a dozen lines.

The language itself is basically Hebrew with a few idiosyncracies. The Samaritans also made extensive use of Aramaic (many texts are bilingual) and both the Hebrew and Aramaic are written in Samaritan script. Since the Muslim invasion, the everyday language of the Samaritans has been Arabic and many of their works appear in Arabic translation, usually in Arabic characters, although sometimes the Arabic is written in Samaritan characters. Instructions in liturgical texts are most frequently written in Arabic.

A wide range of literary types is found. Most works are either copies of Pentateuchs or liturgies, but there are also theological treatises, astrological works, chronicles, and grammars. The liturgical literature in particular is quite extensive with a large number of hymns from different time periods.

The literature reveals influences from the religious literature of those faiths with whom the Samaritans were in most direct contact: Judaism, Christianity, and Islam. The influence of Judaism would be most difficult to document because logic would suggest, and the Samaritans would insist, that any similarities reflect their common origin rather than any continuing influence. The evidence of borrowings from Christianity is most clearly seen in the similarity of the gospel accounts of Jesus and the terms used at times by the Samaritans to talk about Moses (MacDonald 1963: xviii-xix). In literary forms the links with Islam are the most obvious. There is the introductory phrase at the beginning of several units: "In the name of God . . ." often followed by one of his attributes like "the merciful," in agreement with Muslim usage. There are lists of names for God and heaven that parallel very closely Muslim lists. Poetic styles and occasional specific prayers are borrowed from the Muslim heritage.

Significance of Samaritan Studies

Despite articles like John Bowman's "The Importance of Samaritan Researches" (1958-59: 43-54) and statements at the conclusion of encyclopedia articles on the Samaritans to the effect that Samaritan studies are in their infancy and have much to contribute, motivation to do such studies is largely lacking. The reasons are certainly understandable and may be justifiable. The Samaritans represent a small, and so far as any external sources indicate, an insignificant sect. They did not produce a particularly exciting or colorful culture, at least not one that continues to be visible. Their treatises are not brillant; their marginal notes reveal little of intellectual acumen or human interest. The inflated honorific titles by which they identified one another in their bills of sale, often doubling the length of the text, have a transparency through which a materially and intellectually deprived people become visible. The elaboration of ornamentation in their scriptures implies a community preoccupied with the superfluous. A rather colorless, unimaginative community does not sustain the fascination or dedication of scholars.

Nevertheless the Samaritans can be attractive. Bowman points out that the Samaritans are a contemporary vestige of many aspects of ancient Hebrew religion, their practices are rooted in the priestly sacrifices that disappeared in Judaism with the destruction of the temple and the priesthood itself is a remnant of the priests of Zadok. Their Pentateuchal text represents an independent witness between the Masoretic text and the Septuagint. Qumran studies reveal a link between the Samaritans and the Dead Sea community that could illuminate both. Through their eyes we may catch new glimpses of the rise and development of Islam, turbulence in the Middle East during the Crusades, and the Mongol invasion.

There is also a tenacity about this people that commands attention. If the barber of Frederick the Great can respond to the emperor's demand for a proof for the existence of God with the exclamation, "Your majesty, the Jews!" the perpetuity of the Samaritans warrants similar awe. The artifacts they have accumulated are hard to ignore: beautifully printed manuscripts, finely crafted silver inlaid scroll cases, and neatly done inscriptions. Many doors open to history, theology, textual criticism, religious practices and anthropology. The Chamberlain-Warren collection adds several items to the evidence with which we may work.

THE PENTATEUCHS

The Samaritan Pentateuch

Modern Europe had its first glimpse of a Samaritan manuscript in 1616 when Pietro della Valle brought one from Damascus. At present about one hundred pentateuchal manuscripts dating before the present century are listed in various catalogs. A few, like the Abischua scroll in Nablus, are in scroll form which was probably the original form. Most are in codex or book form. The most recent are written on paper, but the earlier ones are written on animal skin.

Although there is consistency within a manuscript, the size of the margins, lines per page or letters per line seem to be left to the judgment of individual scribes rather than prescribed by any canons for copyists. The text itself is written in majuscule characters. The left hand margin is customarily preserved by placing the last letter or two of a line at the appropriate place on the left margin and spacing the remainder of the line so that necessary gaps occur in the middle of the line rather than at the margin. The text is divided into paragraphs, קצים (*qsym*), punctuated at the end by a double dot and a dash -: or some more elaborate variation. Usually a blank space is left between *qsym* although it is not unusual for the last word of a *qsh* to run over that space.

The major punctuation within a *qsh* is the double vertical dot : signifying the end of a sentence. Double horizontal dots ¨ are used as subdividers within the sentence, for direct address and other breaks. Other signs are used for questions: c̈, ⸲, c̣, ⸴, c:, <:; vowel values ¯, �’, ·, ´; and accent. In the Pentateuch larger units of reading are separated by various signs, often a simple bar ⊢⊣.

The Samaritan manuscripts cannot be divided into family groups with anything like the facility that New Testament manuscripts are divided into alpha, beta, gamma, and delta groups. Von Gall despaired: ". . . to construct a family tree of manuscripts as I had earlier thought to do is impossible" (1914-1918: lxviii). Differences between texts seem primarily to reflect the idiosyncracies of a scribe rather than different textual traditions. Availability of more texts and a review of the question do not basically alter his conclusions. I attempted two basic methods of uncovering a pattern. The first was simply to correlate the frequency with which any given manuscript agreed with another manuscript on an alternate reading in von Gall's text. I also checked the number of *qsym* attributed to the books in each manuscript. The second method was to note each instance where a corrector had altered a reading in each of the Chamberlain-Warren manuscripts and to record the manuscripts that supported each, the text and the corrector.

Both methods turned up essentially the same data. A family of manuscripts with significant established support cannot be defined. Nevertheless there were two basic groupings which provide a working hypothesis. The first group includes all three of the Chamberlain-Warren manuscripts plus the manuscripts designated in von Gall as C, H, I, N, P, X, and Q. It happens that three sets of manuscripts by a single scribe turn up in the group: H and P, Q, N, and I, 2478a and 2474, which supports the integrity of the group but does not reduce it to a self defined group. If we can assume that other manuscripts by the same scribes would have a similar text, the group could be expanded to include

Sassoon 403 and 404, Ben-Zvi's ל and לח and von Gall's gothic R and gothic P for a total of 16 manuscripts. Most of these manuscripts were produced in Egypt or southern Palestine in the 15th century A.D.

The other group includes von Gall's A, B, G, gothic A, gothic B, and gothic G and by implication those copied by the father of G as well as V, whose scribe also did A and B. That combination, A, B, and V, is the only instance of common copyists in this group. Manuscript A behaves very strangely in any collation, a fact which I suspect is accounted for by von Gall's usage of it as a ground text for his work. He does not acknowledge this, but A is by far the least cited as containing variants or, to say it the other way, A most often agrees with von Gall's text. This group is much less stable internally than the first group. The majority of these manuscripts were done in Damascus or Shechem in the 14th century, earlier in time and closer geographically to the Samaritan center at Nablus.

A second way of dividing the manuscripts is by geography. Of the 46 manuscripts whose geographical origins can be known with any certainty, all but 6 come from one of four centers: Damascus, Egypt, Zarepath, and Shechem. Seventeen come from Damascus, almost twice as many as from any other place. If we can assume that the community must have had sufficient stability to make their sale profitable, we may infer that Damascus was, generally speaking, a tranquil and prosperous site of the Samaritan *diaspora* over a period of several centuries, for the spread of dates among these manuscripts suggests that Damascus had a rather continuous Samaritan community in exile.

Egypt was the home of the prolific Munes family, a family that produced the largest number of known manuscripts. This productivity occured mainly between 1468 and 1509, a period of 41 years. The surge of manuscript copying in

Egypt may have been part of the fruit of a century of peace beginning with the death of Timurlane in 1404 and the subsequent collapse of Mongol rule. The end of the productivity may witness the suppression of the Samaritan community in Egypt and elsewhere when the Ottoman Turks finally crushed the Mameluke dynasty in 1517.

That Shechem produced a fair share of manuscripts is not surprising since it was the chief Holy Place of the Samaritans. That more were not produced attests to the turbulance of that community and the necessity of frequent and extensive dispersions to other places, notably Egypt and Damascus.

The most unexpected geographical evidence is the appearance of seven manuscripts by scribes associated with Zarepath, all produced in a 65 year period between 1160 and A.D. 1225. Zarepath was located between Tyre and Sidon on the Mediterranean coast. The attraction of this city, which was presumably involved in the intrigues among Syrians, Egyptians and Crusaders, raises another issue regarding the Samaritans for which there is no obvious datum. James Pritchard has found no evidence of Samaritans in his archeological research at Zarepath.

The last attempt at surveying the distribution of Samaritan manuscripts was chronological. If we take the scribal dating as accurate, the earliest dated manuscript apart from the Abischua scroll is that identified as ד by Ben-Zvi and dated 1065. The peak of distribution is reached in the 14th and 15th centuries. There is a noticeably sparse and a noticeably fruitful period.

From the ninety years between 1231 and 1321, not a single manuscript survives. That fact may be silent testimony to the turmoil and atrocities perpetrated in the struggle between Crusaders, Mongols, Mamelukes, and Arabs. The year 1229 marks the curious crusade of Frederick II. In 1252 the Mamelukes defeated the Ayyubids. In

1249 the Mongols entered and the rest of the century was spent in a sustained ouster of Mongols and Crusaders. Samaritans, whether in Shechem or cities of the *diaspora*, experienced their darkest hour since Justinian.

In contrast, the most prosperous period seems to have been reached at the end of the 15th century. An eleven year period between 1474 and 1485 produced an unusual number of manuscripts. If Damascus was the *place* of greatest security for the Samaritans, the late 15th century was the *time* of greatest security for them.

CW 2473

Pentateuch
Samaritan
Animal skin
347 pp.
30.5 x 38 cm.
Test: 22.2 x 28 cm.
34 lines
28 letters per line
Two letter (The existence of this manuscript is noted by Ben-Zvi 1943b: 313-14)

Description. The binding threads have disappeared leaving this manuscript in the form of 16 loose fascicles and, particularly at the beginning and end, several loose pages. The first page of text is on the *verso* of the first leaf. Page two, on the *recto* of the second leaf, is on the hair side of the vellum. There is no evidence of any patching or later repair work. No pagination has been added at any time; page numbers indicated in the following description will not be found in the manuscript itself. There is no binding and consequently many pages are tattered. The letters on a few pages have been written over at some later time (pp. 12, 16, 20, 171, and 337, in particular).

Guidelines so lightly scribed that some are indiscernible have been made vertically for the margins and horizonally for the text. The letters are neatly done in a flat black ink. On a few pages (274, 309, and 326) the ink has eaten completely through the vellum, causing small holes the shape of the letters. The columnar effect whereby the scribe tried to line up words or letters in a vertical column is apparent on almost every page. Very few pages are without at least one set of three letters and some pages have long pronounced columns (pp. 34, 58, 112, 156, 167, 183, 232, 262, and 283). Perhaps one page in twenty has a word or letter extending into the margin. Interlinear corrections are more infrequent than marginal corrections. There are also more than 60 instances of erasure and correction.

Considering the usual care and deference shown to the writing of the divine tetragram (Robertson 1937: 253-54), it is surprising to find two glaring errors in this text. On 193 the sacred name was inadvertently omitted in verse 3. Later it was inserted in the right margin and then the ink was smudged. On 17 the tetragram has been misspelled and the missing letter ' is added above the line.

The *qṣym* are separated by a blank line, although occasionally a single word or two may be placed in the separating line. The punctuation at the end of a *qṣh* has the general pattern - ·· : c :, but the number of times the pattern is repeated varies throughout the text. An even greater diversity exists in the patterns of the same symbols run horizontally across the page to separate larger sections of the Pentateuchal books (for example, at the end of Gen 3, 16, 20, 28, Exod 11, 18, 24, 31:17, and 35:3). The single dot follows every word except at the end of a line and the colon is the major divider within the *qṣh*. Occasionally a horizontal or vertical dash follows the colon and the twin dot is used

12

sparingly as a subdivider, particularly as a sign of direct quotation after a form of the verb אמר, to say. Vocalization marks are comparatively rare. At the conclusion of each book horizontal lines in various patterns decorate the page. In addition to dots, commas, and dashes an interwoven pattern of zigzag lines is common. Into this pattern the word זאת is woven at the end of Genesis, the letter ז at the end of Exodus, א at the end of Leviticus and ז at the end of Numbers. In the margin to the left of every line of text on p. 84 the sign ⊸ .: c: c: appears. The biblical verses at this point are the last 10 verses of the book of Genesis.

Despite extensive weathering and wear, the text is almost complete. The first leaf, pp. 2 and 3, was subjected to a chemical that contracted an area in the center, causing wrinkles across the whole page. Pp. 16 and 18 are also noticeably wrinkled. Most of the pages have some degree of light red splotching and small red dots. Some pages bear large smudges, in a few cases apparently due to kissing and caressing the text. Such instances occur, for example, on pp.

119 and 298, the two appearances of the ten commandments, on p. 224 where the priestly benediction is found and on p. 260 where in Num 25:10 the Aaronic line traced through Phineas is guaranteed a perpetual priesthood. Holes of various sizes, from small worm holes to 3 inch circular skin blemishes, are fairly common. Five tears averaging around 5 inches each have been sewn (pp. 42, 52, 70, 108, 186). Most of the large holes and all of the tears were in the skins before the text was written.

There has been little later tampering with the text, although someone later preferred fuller readings and such additions as the underlined letter in the words ואבי Gen 17:4, חאפיכה Gen 19:29, בית Gen 28:2 are common.

Date and scribe. Two *tashqil* or acrostics are contained within the manuscript. At the ח in זבח in Lev 7:11 the acrostic חצי התורה ("Half of the Torah") begins. It ends with the ה in נדבה in verse 16. The major acrostic begins with the א in אמר in Lev 21:1 and ends with the ה in געלה in 26:43. It reads:

(1) אני . שת . אהרון . בן . יצחק . בן . שת . אהרון . כהנה . חירא . וזקן . צלותה . בדמשק . כתבת .

(2) זאת . התורה . הקדושה . לסהבה . וסמוך . קהלה . וארכונה . אב . קויתי . בן . סהבה . וסמוך .

(3) קהלה . וארכונה . ושמור . ארהותה . אבי . הפתח . דמבני . מטר . בשנת . ארבע . ושבעים .

(4) ושמנה . מאות . לממלכת . ישמעאל . תהיה . בריכה . עליו .

(1) "I, Seth Ahron son of Isaak son of Seth Ahron the priest (..) (..) (..) at Damascus; I wrote
(2) this holy Torah for (..) (..) (..) Ab Quwait son of (..) (..)
(3) (..) (..) Abu'l Fatch (Ab Happetach) of the family Matar, in the year 874
(4) of the reign of the Ishmaelites (A.D. 1470). May there be a blessing upon him."

Each bracketed pair of dots represents an honorific title which the Samaritans used generously. Their precise meaning is not always clear (Robertson 1937: 260).

The name of this scribe appears in a few other manuscripts. One designated C by von Gall (1914-18: iv) was written in A.D. 1481 and is presently in the Bibliotheque nationale in Paris. He was a witness to a bill of sale in 1446/7 (von Gall 1914-18: lxxiv) and the writer of another bill of sale in 1469 (von Gall 1914-18: xxii). The son of Seth Ahron produced the manuscript designated gothic C in von Gall and dated A.D. 1504 (von Gall 1914-18: xxx).

Bill of Sale. When a manuscript exchanged hands a bill of sale was frequently written within the manuscript itself at the end of one of the biblical books where there was extra space on the page. CW 2473 contains only one bill of sale located at the end of the book of Leviticus. It reads:

(1) קנא . זאת . התורה ׃ הקדושה . סהבה . וסמוך .

(2) קה ; וארכ ;קה ; ויק ; וקר ; וצל ; וחש ; וכתובה .

(3) ונאי ; ויד ; ומב ; ועשה . טבאתה . יעקב . בן .

(4) סהבה . וסמ ; קה ; ואר ; קה ; ויק ; וקר ; וצ ; וע ;

(5) טב ; אברהמ . <u>מבני</u> . פוקה . המצרי . מן . סהבה . וס ;

(6) קה ; וא ; קה ; ויק ; וקר ; וצל ; וח ; וכת ; ועשה .

(7) טו ; אב . עלי ; בן . סה ; ויק ; וק ; וצל ; וסמוך .

(8) קה ; ואר ; קה ; אב . סכו ; בן . אבי ; הפתח ; דמבני .

(9) מטר . בשלשים . דנר . זהב . בחדש . שואל ׳שנת .

(10) אחד . עשר . ותשע . מאות . לממ ; ישמ ; תהיה .

(11) בריכה . עליו . וילמד . בה . בנימ . ובני . בנ .

(12) אמנ . אמנ . בעמל . משה . חנא מ ן .

(1) This Holy Torah was bought by (..) (..)

(2) (..) (..) (..) (..) (..) (..) (..) (..)

(3) (..) (..) (..) (..) (..) Jakob son of

(4) (..) (..) (..) (..) (..) (..) (..) (..) (..)

(5) (..) Abraham of the family Puqah, the Egyptian, from (..) (..)

(6) (..) (..) (..) (..) (..) (..) (..) (..) (..)

(7) (..) Ab Elyon son of (..) (..) (..) (..) (..)

(8) (..) (..) (..) Ab Sekuah son of Abu'l Fatch of the family

(9) Matar for thirty gold dinars in the month of Shawwal in the year

(10) 911 of the reign of the Ishmaelites (A.D. 1505) May there be

(11) a blessing upon it and may it instruct children and grandchildren.

(12) Amen. Amen. Through the merit of Moses the faithful.

The new owner, Jakob son of Abraham, had apparently bought the manuscript from the nephew of the man for whom it was originally written. In 1479 the same Jakob bought another manuscript, now known as Codex II of the John Rylands Library at Manchester (Robertson 1938: col. 28) and in 1518 he bought the manuscript numbered 14 in the catalogue of Ben Zvi (1943a: 413). The sellers,

Ab Elyon and members of his family, are also mentioned in other transactions involving Samaritan manuscripts: in 1546 he was the buyer of manuscript N listed in von Gall (1914-18: xviii-xix); he is the scribe of manuscript X (1914-18: xxiv-xxv); one of his sons bought three manuscripts cited by von Gall (1914-18: xxxi-xxxii); another son, apparently, was the seller in 1586 of manuscript R (1914-18: lxxv); and finally a grandson was the buyer of manuscript gothic K (1914-18: lxxx) and was the witness in a sale of manuscript X cited above.

Two witnesses have verified the bill of sale. The first states:

(1) סהד . במה . סופיר

(2) יוסף . בן . אהרן

(3) בן . יעקב . בן . ישמ ;

(4) והכתב . על . פיו

(1) A witness to what is written:

(2) Joseph son of Ahron

(3) son of Jakob son of Ismael

(4) and it was written as he says.

The other witness wrote:

(1) סהדתי . במה . סופ ;

(2) וכתב . אברהם . בן .

(3) עבד . יהוה . חבתה .

(4) בדמשק . יה ; יכ ;

(5) חטא ;

(1) I am a witness of what is declared

(2) and written: Abraham son of

(3) Obadiah the "second priest"

(4) in Damascus. May Yahweh forgive

(5) (his) sins.

He is probably the same person mentioned as the recipient of gothic J in 1509/10 according to von Gall (for the title "second priest" see Cowley 1909: lv).

Other Colophons and Additions. There are several other brief colophons. The end of each book bears a record of the number of *qsym*.

Genesis	ספר . הראישרן .
(250)	קצים . ר . ו . ך
Exodus	ספר . השני .
(200)	ר .: קצים
Leviticus	הספר . השלישי -.:
(135)	ק c: והל c: קצה c: -.:
Numbers	ספר . הרביעי -.:
(216)	קצים . ר . ווי c: -.:
Deuteronomy	ספר . החמישי .
(166)	קצים . ק . ; וס . ; וו ;

The number of *qsym* for the first 3 books conforms with the majority of manuscripts cited in von Gall (1914-18: lxiii). For Numbers and Deuteronomy, CW 2473 has a unique number. In the right margin of p. 46 there is a design, very likely a word, pricked through the vellum with a sharp point. The word is illegible. At the end of Genesis the word אוה[ה] has been crudely scratched into the vellum.

Seven colophons, five in Samaritan and two in Arabic, appear on the last two pages. One of the Samaritan colophons asks that the peace of Yahweh be upon Moses, the rest witness to the accuracy of the text:

(1) ושלום . יהוה . על . משה . בן . עמרם

(2) תורה . תמימה . -.:

ברוך . נותינה .

(3) תמים . תיהי . זה . התורה .

(4) תמים . זה . התורה . הקדושה .

(5) תמים . תי .

הי . זה .

התורה .

(1) "The peace of Yahweh be upon Moses the son of Aaron"

(2) "A complete Torah, blessed be its giver"

(3) "This Torah is complete"

(4) "This Holy Torah is complete"

(5) "This Torah is complete"

The fifth colophon, with the exception of the last word, is enclosed in a small box formed with zigzag lines. Two later, but undated, Arabic colophons are found on the last page. They attest that the text is "without error" and ask blessings upon the writer.

CW 2478a

Pentateuch
Samaritan and Arabic
Animal Skin
484 Pp. 32.5 x 38 cm.
Text: 28 x 23 cm.
41 Lines
17 Letters in each of two columns per line
Two Letter

Introduction. The most pretentious of the three fifteenth century A.D. manuscripts in the Chamberlain-Warren collection is CW 2478a, labeled the "Murjan Manuscript" on its wrapping. According to the note affixed to it during its stay in the museum in Three Oaks, MI, it is the oldest and most expensive manuscript in the collection. The note, typed by the Three Oaks museum staff, dated the manuscript A.D. 1200 and stated that Mr. Warren paid $1500 for it. Mr. Warren's son later claimed it was a gift. It was the only manuscript labeled by name and although (or perhaps because) the significance of the name was lost by the time the book reached Three Oakes, the fact that it had a name implied to the new owner that it was special.

In consideration of a letter uncovered by

Professor Purvis in the W. E. Barton collection in the Boston University library, it seems likely that the name is inherited from the last Samaritan owner, Salamah Murjan, who in effect pawned the manuscript with the American Samaritan Committee. The letter written by Warren's brother-in-law, F. W. Chamberlain, to Mr. Barton on June 8, 1921, reads in part:

John Whiting writes that Salloum Murjan is unable to redeem the old manuscript which had an approximate value of $1000. Whiting has therefore paid him the amount that was due on the purchase price, and the manuscript is our property. Murjan requests a further extension which Whiting transmits, but at the same time adds that he doubts whether Murjan will be any more able to buy this manuscript back later than he is now.

The manuscript was probably labeled, "Murjan Manuscript" for practical identification should he decide to redeem it. Although he was never in a financial position to reclaim his property, his name continued to be associated with it. It is perhaps the same Murjan who was a witness to the sale of Sassoon manuscript 403 in 1903 and is mentioned in a note in Sassoon manuscript 404 (Sassoon 1932: 581). An undated note in one of the treatises in the John Rylands collection records the birth of a son to a Salamah ben Murjan (Robertson 1938: 129).

The manuscript was probably sent to the museum in Three Oaks in 1921 (Purvis 1972: 12). The bulk of the Chamberlain-Warren Samaritan materials were shipped from Jerusalem in July, 1920, according to an invoice dated July 23rd of that year. But it describes only two parchment manuscripts and the description offered by Barton in a letter dated November 30, 1920, fits the two other manuscripts in the collection, CW 2473 and CW 2484, implying that Professor Purvis is right in assuming that CW 2478a was sent at the later date.

Description. CW 2478a contains 484 pp. gathered into 17 fascicles. Unlike CW 2473 or CW 2484 in which the left and right pages at any opening in the codex would either both be the hair side or the flesh side of the skin, CW 2478a breaks this rhythm on pp. 35-36, 47-48, 271-272, 403-404 and 415-416. Several pages are noticeably thinner than the average: 216, 280, 282, 290, 292, 302 and 412. Page 1 is written on the flesh side. Binding threads of white or gold hold the manuscript together. Pp. 448-449 were folded in the wrong place before binding. Extensive patches have been made in the margins throughout the text, but there are no covers. No pagination has been added and page numbers referred to in this text do not appear in the manuscript.

Horizontal lines for the text and vertical lines for the margins have been inscribed with a sharp tool. In the Arabic columns the left line is terminated at the margin and excess letters are written further to the left. Robertson notes the same phenomenon in his description of Codices II and III (1938: 18,34). The letters are written in a flat black ink and are generally very neat. An occasional page shows crowding (e.g. 83 and 105), excessive smudging or irregular lines (e.g. 181 and 282). There are a few instances of ink eating through the page (46, 312 and 334). Columns of letters or words characteristic of Samaritan manuscripts in general are far less common in bilingual texts such as this one and only a few pages have outstanding examples of columns (e.g. 18, 20 and 25). There are

frequent interlinear additions or corrections and more than half the pages bear evidence of erasure. Occasionally (more than 25 times in Genesis) the correction is in an obviously different hand and it is usually clear that the corrector is expressing his preference for an alternate rendering of the text rather than correcting a careless error. On p. 456 there is a long correction written vertically up the center margin in a striking hand. It is rare for the Hebrew text to violate the margin. Several pages contain lines that have been written over at a later time: 1, 5, 74, 102, 148, 152, 269, 302, 331, 343, 355, 357, 375, 379, 413. Pp. 5 and 74 have been carelessly overwritten.

The *qsym* are usually separated by a blank line although frequently a single word or two may be placed on the separating line. The punctuation at the end of the *qsym* is -:. Larger units of the Pentateuch are marked off by a short horizonal line ⊢⊣ standing alone on a line. Such signs appear through Genesis, for example, at the end of 6:16, 19:18, 23:20, 38:30 and 39:34. .:⊢⊣:. stands at the end of Gen 38:30, Exod 11:10, Lev 15:33, Num 6:21, 15:21, 25:9 and Deut 16:17. The conclusion of a book is marked by a series of c.:⊢⊣c.: extending from margin to margin.

About ten percent of the pages contain circular holes from 1.5-8.0 cm. in diameter, apparently caused by blemishes in the animal skin. Most of these are in the margin. When they appear in the text the scribe plans his text around them. Worm holes and other irregular tears occur less frequently. On p. 392 a 5 cm. tear has been sewn. Many stains appear throughout the text and most of them can be identified as either smudged glue used in applying patches or ink.

Date and Scribe. Two *tashqil* are contained within the manuscript. The first, on p. 235 is

the acrostic חצי התורה (Half of the Torah) beginning with the ח in זבח in Lev 7:16. The
usual bar separating the two words is missing.

The major acrostic begins with the א in יביאך
in Deut 6:10 and concludes with the ם in וביום
in Deut 16:8. It reads:

(1) אני . עפיף . בן . צדקה . בן . יעקב . בן . צדקה .

(2) בן . אב . חסדה . בן . עבד . יהוה . דמבני . מוניס .

(3) הכתוב . במצרים . כתבתי . זאת . התורה .

(4) הקדושה . על . שם . סהבה . ויקירה .

(5) ואקר . טוב . וקראה . וצלאה . וחשובה .

(6) וכתובה . וסמוך . קהלה . וארכון .

(7) קהלה . ועשה . טובה . עבד . היהוב .

(8) בן . סמוכה . רבה . וארכונה . ומסכינה .

(9) יוסף . בן . זקנה . טבה . אב . תחמדתה .

(10) דמבני . איקרה . יהוה . ישימה . מברכה .

(11) עליו . וילמד . בה . בנים . ובני . בנים .

(12) אמן . שנת . ט . ופ . וח . ק . לממלכת . בני .

(13) ישמעאל . והיא . מליו . א . ול . תורה . כתבתי .

(14) מודאה . לאלה . לבדו . עורה . מן . זבח .

(15) מצרים .

(1)   I, Aphiph son of Sedaqa son of Jakob son of Sedaqa
(2)   son of Ab Chisda son of Obadiah of the family Munes
(3)   am the writer in Egypt. I wrote this Holy Torah
(4)   for (..) (..)
(5)   (..) (..) (..) (..) (..)
(6)   (..) (..) (..) (..)
(7)   (..) (..) (..) Abd Hehob
(8)   son of (..) (..) (..) (..)
(9)   Joseph son of (..) (..) Ab Tachamdata
(10) of the family of Iqara. May Yahweh put a blessing
(11) upon it and may it instruct children and grandchildren.
(12) Amen. It is the year 889 of the reign of the sons of
(13) Ishmael (A.D. 1484) and this is the 31st Torah.I have written.
(14) Thanks be to God alone. Upon skins from the altar in
(15) Egypt.

The Munes family in Egypt to which Aphiph belonged is known from more than a dozen members of the family who were scribes or witnesses in the 15th and 16th centuries A.D. Aphiph himself was the scribe of four known manuscripts out of a claimed total of at least 33. They are in chronological order: von Gall's I (881 A.H./ A.D. 1477) (1914-18:xii), Ben-Zvi's לד (A.H. 886/A.D. 1481) (1943c: 17), CW 2478a (A.H. 889/ A.D. 1484) and von Gall's gothic P (A.H. 890/

A.D. 1485) (1914-18: xli-xlii). They were re-spectively his 19th, 28th, 31st and 33rd. Two other scribes, אב נצענה and אב נצחנה, claim the same geneology as Aphiph and must be considered either as brothers or as aliases. Some of the problems involved in that identification are discussed in the subsequent material on 2484 whose scribe was אב נצחנה (see below). My conclusion is that we are dealing with one scribe under three names and, therefore, 2478a and 2484 are by the same scribe. The recipient of CW 2478a is otherwise unknown, nor does anyone else by this name appear in Samaritan lists. Some of the names, in different form, appear in the problematic third bill of sale in manuscript I (von Gall, 1914-18: xiii-xiv). It is problematic because the date is uncertain; הטוב appears as a name in place of היהוב and Tachamadata is of the family of Amkara rather than Iqara.

Bills of Sale. There are four bills of sale. Taken in chronological order, the first appears at the end of Exodus. It reads:

(1) קני . זאת . התורה . הקדושה . סמוך . קהלה . וארכון .

(2) קהלה . יוסף . בן . סהבה . וסמוך . קהלה . ועשה . טובה .

(3) עבד . יהוה . בן . עבד . היהוב . דמבני . איקרה . מן . סהבה .

(4) וסמוך . קהלה . וארכון]. קהלה . ויעדוה . ועשה . טובה .

(5) עבד . יהוה . בן . סהבה . וסמוך . וקהלה . ועשה . טובה .

(6) עבד . היהוב . בן . צדקה . דמבני . רמח . וכהלון . מן .

(7) שכוני . מצרים . בארבעה . ועשרים . דנר . בחדש . רגב . שנת .

(8) שנים . ותשעים . ושמנה . מאות . תהיה . בריכה . עליו . אמן .

(9) וכתב . אברהם . בן . אבי . עזי . בן . יוסף . בן . יתרנה .
מן . דמשך .

(1) This Holy Torah was bought by (..) (..) (..)

(2) (..) Joseph son of (..) (..) (..) (..) (..)

(3) Obadiah son of Abd Hehob of the family of Iqara from (..)

(4) (..) (..) (..) (..) (..) (..) (..)

(5) Obadiah son of (..) (..) (..) (..) (..)

(6) Abd Hehob son of Sedaqa of the family Remach, all of them from

(7) among the inhabitants of Egypt for 24 dinars in the month of Rajab in the year

(8) 892 (A.D. 1487). May there be a blessing upon it. Amen.

(9) Abraham son of Ab Uzzi son of Joseph son of Jitrana of Damascus wrote this.

The manuscript is apparently being repur-chased by the Iqara family, but it is not stated how the manuscript passed from the hands of Abd Hehob of the Iqara family, the grandfather of the present buyer, into the hands of Obadiah of the Remach family. The latter is not unknown to us. In A.H. 867 (A.D. 1463) Obadiah bought gothic F (von Gall 1914-18: xxxiv) and he wrote a poetic note in another manuscript that he owned (von Gall 1914-18: xx-xxi). The buyer is a more ob-scure figure, but he is possibly the Joseph son of Abdullah who ten years later bought gothic F from another member of the Remach family (von Gall 1914-18: xxxv). The writer of the bill of

sale is otherwise unknown to us. The fact that
he is from Damascus is a witness to the mobility
of the Samaritans of the *diaspora*.

At the end of Leviticus a second bill of
sale reads:

(1) קני . זאת . התורה . הקדושה . במה . דהלו . לנפשו .

(2) סהבה . טבה . וסמ ; קה ; ואר ; קה ; ויק ; ואקר ; טוב . וקר ;

(3) רץ ; וחש ; ובת ; וייעד ; ועשה . טובה ; אברהם . בן . סהבה .

(4) טבה . וסמ ; קה ; ואר ; קה ; ומסכינה . עבדיה . דמבני .

(5) התנך . מן . שהלא ; ושתיתה ; ילידי . סהבה . טבה . ומס ;

(6) קה ; ואר ; קה ; זיק ; ואקר . טוב . וקר ; רץ ; והש ; וך ;

(7) וייעד ; וזקין . ישראל . ושמור ; ארחותה . קדישתה .

(8) ועשה . טבהתה . ומסכינה . יוסף . בן . סהבה . טבה . וסמ ;

(9) קה ; ואר ; קה ; ומסכינה . עבד . אלה . בן . יהובה . דמבני .

(10) איקרה . והיא . מורשה . להם מן . אברהם . הווכיר . יסלח .

(11) לו . יה ; וישכון . רוחו . בגנה . ומכרתם . ונתן . להם .

(12) בידם . מנחתהם . שנים . ועשרים . דנר . זהב . מצרי . ואסיד .

(13) על . נפשותם . אן . לית . להם . בזהת . התורה . קשט . וכן . בירח .

(14) גמאדי . אלאול . שנת   חמש . שנים . ותשע . מאות . לממלכות .

(15) ישמעאל . וכן . אסיד . וכתב . עבד . רחמנה . בן . עבד . אלה .

(16) בן . עבד . יהובה . אחי . אביהם . הזוכיר . תהיה . בריכה .

(17) ומברכה . עליו . אמן . בעמל . משה . הנחמן .

(1)   This Holy Torah was bought with his own money for himself
(2)   by (..) (..) (..) (..) (..) (..) (..) (..) (..) (..)
(3)   (..) (..) (..) (..) (..) (..) Abraham son of (..)
(4)   (..) (..) (..) (..) (..) (..) Obadiah of the family
(5)   Hattanak from Shahala and Shatithah, children of (..) (..) (..)
(6)   (..) (..) (..) (..) (..) (..) (..) (..) (..) (..)
(7)   (..) (..) (..) (..) (..) (..)
(8)   (..) (..) (..) Joseph son of (..) (..) (..)
(9)   (..) (..) (..) (..) Abdullah son of Jehuba of the family of
(10)   Iqara. It was an inheritance to them from Abraham. May Yahweh esteem his
        memory and
(11)   cause his spirit to dwell in the garden. And they sold it and he gave them,
(12)   in their hands, the sum of 22 gold Egyptian dinars. I witness
(13)   on their behalf what is theirs in this true Torah. It is the month of
(14)   Jomada I in the year 905 of the reign of
(15)   the Ishmaelites (A.D. 1500) and I, Abd Rachmana son of Abdullah
(16)   son of Abd Jehuba, brother of their father, whose memory is a blessing
        witnessed and wrote this.
(17)   May there be a blessing upon it. Amen. Through the merit of Moses the
        faithful.

Appropriately the children of the previous buyer are the sellers in this contract. The girls are otherwise unknown. It is not clear why they inherited the manuscript from Abraham rather than from their father. They had a grandfather, Abraham (father of Sedaqa in von Gall's gothic F and himself the recipient of manuscripts לד and לט in Ben Zvi) (Ben-Zvi 1943c:17, 19) and an uncle Abraham (the seller of gothic L in von Gall). However, it is not easy to surmise why either of these men, with sons of their own, would will a Torah to a granddaughter or niece. A maternal grandfather or uncle would be a more likely possibility, but since the manuscript was the possession of the father by the previous bill of sale, it may be best to assume a deceased brother by the name of Abraham. Neither the buyer nor the witness is otherwise known. The buyer is the father of the seller in the next bill of sale and the witness and scribe is the uncle of the girls.

In A.H. 928 (A.D. 1522) a third bill of sale was recorded at the end of Genesis. It reads:

(1) קנה . זאת . התורה . הקדשה .
(2) סהבה . טבה . ושמור . אהרות .
(3) קדיש . יוסף . בן . סהבה .
(4) אברהם . בן . סהבה . ומס ;
(5) צדקה . דמבני . יוסף .
(6) הגררי . מן . סמוכה . רבה .
(7) יוסף . בן . סה ; ומס . אברהם .
(8) בן . סה ; ומס ; עבד . אלה .
(9) דמבני . התנך . ומצרי .
(10) רמנ חתה . ארבע . עשר . דנר .
(11) ואנפל . קשטו . מן . התובו .
(12) רזאת . וקנין . קשט . וכן .
(13) בחדש . רביע . השני . שנת .
(14) ח : רכ ∵: רט ∵: מאות .
(15) וכן . אסיד . וכתבו . עבד .
(16) הטוב . בן . יעקב . בן .
(17) חכומה . אב . עליון . דמבני .

(18) רמח . יסלח . לו . יה ;
(19) אמן . בעמל . משה . הנאמן .

(1)   This Holy Torah was bought by
(2) (..) (..) (..) (..)
(3) (..) Joseph son of (..)
(4) Abraham son of (..) (..)
(5) Sedaqa of the family of Joseph
(6) the Gerarite from (..) (..)
(7) Joseph son of (..) (..) Abraham
(8) son of (..) (..) Abdullah
(9) of the family of Hattanak in Egypt
(10) and its price was 14 dinars.
(11) And if truth falls (from the mouth of) his she-ass
(12) may this one acquire truth and uprightness.
(13) In the month of Rabia II in the year
(14) 928 (A.D. 1522).
(15) I, Abd
(16) Hattob, son of Jakob son of
(17) (..) Ab Elyon of the family
(18) Remach, witnessed and wrote this. Yahweh have mercy upon him.
(19) Amen. Through the merit of Moses the faithful.

The seller, who is known to us as the buyer of Sassoon 403 in A.H. 938 (A.D. 1532) (Sassoon 1932: 582), is the son of the previous buyer. Through the time of this sale the manuscript remained in Egypt. The buyer is a member of a family from Gerar. Again the destiny of gothic F intersects with CW 2478a: the new owner was the buyer of gothic F a year earlier (von Gall 1914-18: xxxiv). There the family name is not clear; von Gall suggests Sehaba, but in this manuscript it is Joseph. In gothic F Joseph is said to come from Gaza, while this document refers to him as a Gerarite. But Gerar was a district as well as a city and the likelihood that

Gaza is within the boundaries of that district makes the identity of these two buyers more, rather than less, likely.

On the page with this bill of sale there are also five attestations to the accuracy of the text, all written in Arabic.

The fourth bill of sale lies at the end of Numbers. It reads:

(1) קנה . זאת . התורה . הקד ; יקר ; וצ ; וחש ; וך ; ון ; ושמ ; וה ;

(2) וס ; קה ; וא ; קה ; ועש ; טב ; אב . קוי ; בן . סה ; ט ; ויק ; וק ; וצ ; וח ; וך ;

(3) וס ; רבה ; וא ; יצחק . בן . סה ; וס ; ר ; וא ; בזז . דמבני . מונס . מן .

(4) ס ; וי ; וק ; וצ ; וחש ; וך ; ויד ; וש ; אה ; קד ; הס ; ר ; וא ; יוסף . בן]. סה ; ר ; וס ;

(5) ר ; וא ; אברהמ]. בן . סה ; ומס ; צדקה . דמבני . הגררי . מן . שכר ;

(6) ארץ ; מצר ; וזה ; הק ; בשלש . מאות . כסף . אד . ומי . בחדש .

(7) שואל . שנת . אחד . ושלשים ; ותשע . מאות . למ ; ישמעאל . תהיה . בר ;

(8) על ; א ; וילמד . ב ; בן ; וב ; בן ; אמן . א ; בעמל . משה . ה ;

(9) אסיד . בכל

(10) וכתבו . אבי

(11) עזי . בן . יוסף

(12) בן . הרבן

(13) איתמר

(14) ובכל . אסיד . וכתבו

(15) יוסף . בן . הרבן . אבי

(16) עזי . בן . איתמר .

(1)   This Holy Torah was bought by (..) (..) (..) (..) (..) (..)
(2)   (..) (..) (..) (..) (..) (..) Ab Quwait son of (..) (..) (..) (..) (..) (..) (..)
(3)   (..) (..) (..) Isaak son of (..) (..) (..) (..) Bazaz of the family of Munes from
(4)   (..) (..) (..) (..) (..) (..) (..) (..) (..) (..) (..) (..) (..) Joseph son of (..) (..) (..)
(5)   (..) (..) Abraham son of (..) (..) Sedaqa of the family Hagerari among the inhabitants of
(6)   the land of Egypt and this was purchased with 300 silver edomites in the month of
(7)   Shawwal in the year 931 of the reign of the Ishmaelites (A.D. 1525). May there be a blessing
(8)   on it. Amen. Through the merit of Moses the faithful.

Robertson identifies "edomites" as Roman coinage.

The note to the right at the bottom reads:

(9)   I am a witness to everything
(10)   and wrote it: Ab

22

(11) Uzzi son of Joseph

(12) son of (..)

(13) Itamar.

The note at the left reads,

(14) And to everything I
witness and write:

(15) Joseph son of (..) Ab

(16) Uzzi son of Itamar.

The seller was appropriately the buyer in the previous bill of sale. The buyer comes from a well-known family, but is himself unknown to us in other manuscripts. The two witnesses are cousins. Their grandfather, Itamar, had at least two sons, Joseph, the father of the present witness, Ab Uzzi (who was also a witness to Ben Zvi's ד״י in A.D. 1509) and a second son, Ab Uzzi who is mentioned as a scribe in a note in von Gall's gothic D in 1532. Joseph, the son of the latter Ab Uzzi was the scribe of that note as well as a bill of sale in von Gall's X in the same year, the present bill of sale in CW 2478a, and another in von Gall's N, undated. Von Gall's comment that it is not impossible that the scribe of N is also the father of the witness Ab Uzzi in Damascus in E may be stated with greater certitude. The latter Ab Uzzi was also a witness to von Gall's V in A.H. 986 (A.D. 1578).

Other Colophons and Additions. There remain a few other colophons and stray words. At the end of Leviticus a later hand has written:

ספר השלישי

ק;ו;ל . קצים

The third book
130 paragraphs

Most manuscripts record 135 divisions for Leviticus. At the end of the manuscript a colophon reads:

תורה . תמימה
ברוך . נתונה

A completed Torah
Blessed be the giver

Under the ב is a rather carelessly written את. Two other stray and cryptic words are found in the text. At the bottom of the page under the bill of sale at the end of Leviticus appears the word ה.[]דב. The letter in the brackets is almost triangular in shape suggesting an ע or a מ. If the last letter could be a פ the word could be עדף suggesting an overflow or excess. There is also a possibility that a dot separates the second and third letters in which case it could be, "The witness . . ." The last isolated word appears in the lower left margin of p. 178 and reads סֹ plus a final character that looks very much like an ampersand (&). The latter character could be an ס but it is not the same as the initial letter. Perhaps it is a form of פ and the word is סוף, the "end".

CW 2478b

Exodus Fragment
Samaritan
Animal Skin
1 Leaf
15.5 x 9 cm.
12-13 Lines
25 Letters per Line
One Letter

Between pp. 147 and 148 of CW 2478a (which begins with Exod 11:5) a fragment from another manuscript was found. It is rather rectangular in shape. The flesh side carries 13 lines and the hair side 12. The passages are Exod 25:27 from the word המסגרת to 32 ending with the נ

n השני and 25:39 beginning with the ו in
שהוו to 26:4 ending with the word במחברת. The
fragment seems to have been intentionally cut
(to be used as a book mark?) with a sharp tool
rather than torn or worn out. Within the body of
the fragment are several slashes with a sharp
line, two of which go completely through the
parchment for a distance of about 5 cm.

In 12 of the lines the words are well spaced
so that the entire last word sits on the left
margin. In 13 lines it is necessary for the
scribe to set up a left margin and in every one
of these cases it is a single letter rather than
two letters that have been placed at the left
margin. This is one argument for an early dating
of this manuscript (Robertson 1938: xxv). An
early date is also supported by the presence of
the separating dot after the words at the end of
a line. Later manuscripts no longer carry this
unnecessary mark. Further there is no indication
of vocalization marks nor any suggestion of
columns of letters or words. The only criterion
of early dating that this fragment fails to meet
is the occasional use of horizontal double dots
as punctuation. Thus this fragment probably
dates a century or two earlier than the other
two Pentateuchs in the collection. A preliminary
survey of other fragments does not readily reveal other portions of this manuscript.

The text is in rather small majuscule
characters and is quite legible, although some of
the letters on the flesh side have faded. The
punctuation at the end of the *qsym* seems to be
simply a colon. There is a brown cast to the
page.

CW 2484

Pentateuch
Samaritan
Animal Skin
427 Pp.
28.3 x 35 cm.
Text: 26 x 18 cm.
33 Lines
24 Letters per Line
Two Letter

Description. CW 2484 is visually unique a-
mong the three 15th century A.D. Pentateuchs in
the Chamberlain-Warren collection because it is
the only one that has been bound in recent times.
After extensive patching of the pages and re-
placement of the first 5 and last 18 pp. the 17
fascicles were bound with white thread and en-
cased in a cover of red napped wool stretched
over cardboard. The binding threads are collected at top and bottom by a braiding of green and
red thread. The back cover extends into a flap
that fits over the front of the manuscript.

The first of the original pages, p. 6, was
written on the hair side of the skin. Throughout the manuscript the left and right pages are
either both the hair side or the flesh side of
the skin. No pagination has been added and the
page numbers referred to in this text do not
appear on the manuscript.

Horizontal lines for the text and vertical
lines for the margins have been inscribed with a
sharp tool. On pp. 358-59 the tool accidentally
made a 1.5 cm. slit in the page. The letters are
written in a flat black ink in a generally neat
hand. On some pages (e.g., 26, 58, 72, 177,
180) the letters are quite crowded. There are
at least 70 erasures in addition to several
words that have been crossed out. Several
letters and some entire lines have been overwritten on pp. 8, 45, 53, 66, 70, 74, 83, and

24

236, occasionally in purple ink (pp. 60, 67). Compared to CW 2473 there is relatively little attempt to arrange letters or words in columns. The ten commandments in Exodus were numbered in the margin by the scribe.

In addition to the pages that have been replaced at the front and back of the manuscript, almost 100 pp. have been patched and half the patches bear writing. A patch on p. 395 has been placed over a portion of the text but the text has not been recopied on the patch. The pages bear a variety of holes caused by worms (90, 92, 96), acid in the ink (36, 40, 166, 192, 373, 384, 390), blemishes in the animal skin (139, 156, 168, 169, 240, 278) and erasures (194, 218, 370). Two series of pages (54-69, 72-85) bear a line of pin pricks along the outside margin. Apparently these pages were either prepared to be sewn together in a scroll or, more likely, erroneously prepared for binding on the wrong margin. The priestly benediction on p. 279 and the passage in Lev 9:22-23:2 on p. 222 are darkened, presumably from being caressed. Three sewn tears appear in the manuscript: a 5 cm. tear on pp. 108-9, a 7.5 cm. tear on pp. 158-59 and a 10 cm. tear on pp. 398-99.

The qsym are usually separated by a blank line, although frequently a single word or two may be placed on the separating line. The punctuation at the end of a qsh is -c:. The sign .:⊢⊣:. appears after Gen 28:22; 33:20; 38:30; Exod 11:10 and 35:3; Lev 9:21 and 22:33; Num 15:41; 25:9 and 30:1. The sign ⊢⊣ appears after Gen 40:23 and 46:7; Exod 17:7; Lev 5:26 and

24:23; Num 1:43; 4:49; 7:83; 19:22; 20:13, 22 and 22:1. The two signs - : c : - and ⊢⊣ ⊢⊣ appear only once, the former after Exod 28:43 and the latter after Num 32:42. The single dot follows every word throughtout the text and the colon is the major divider within the qsym. Vocalization marks the double dot are hardly used at all. The ending of Deuteronomy is missing. The conclusion of Exodus is marked by a horizontally placed zigzag line, each identation carrying a v or a dot. The end of the other three books is delineated by a row of c.: c.: c.:.

A later scribe has made approximately 75 changes in the text. Most of the changes are corrections of spellings or haplography and dittography. A curious oversight of even the corrector is the misspelling of the word "Israel" on p. 151. Many of the changes represent a decided preference for alternate readings. He consistently rejects the readings of CW 2484 that are supported by von Gall's I and is in most common agreement with readings supported by H, N, and P in von Gall.

Date and Scribe. Two *tashqil* are contained within the manuscript. The first, on p. 217 is the acrostic חצי . התורה (Half the Torah) beginning with the ח in זבח in Lev 7:11 and concluding with ה in המקריב in Lev 7:18. The major acrostic begins with the א in יביאך in Deut 6:10 and concludes with the ם in הבנים in Deut 22:6. It reads:

(1) אני . אב . נצחנה . בר . צדקה . בר . יעקב . בר . צדקה .
(2) בר . אב . חסדה . בר . עבד . יהוה . דמבני . מונס . הכתוב .
(3) במצרים . כתבתי . זאת . התורה . הקדושה . לסהבה .
(4) טבה . ויקירה . ואקר . טוב . וקראה . וצלאה . וחשובה .
(5) וכתובה . וסמוך . קהלה . וארכון . קהלה . ועשה . טובה .
(6) ואבי . אלמנה . ויתומה . אבי . רוממתה . בר . סהבה .
(7) טבה . ויקירה . וסמוך . קהלה . וארכונה . ומסכינה .

(8) אברהם . בר . סהבה . וקראה . וסמוך . קהלה . וארכונה .

(9) אבי . רוממתה . דמבני . איקרה . במדלו . לנפשו .

(10) בשלשה . עשר .דינר . יהוה . ישימה . מברכה .

(11) עליו . וילמד . בה . בנים . ובני . בנים . אמן .

(12) בשנת . חוע . ושמנה . מאות . לממלכת . בני .

(13) ישמעאל . והיא . מליו . חי . ארואן . כתבתי .

(14) דאה . לאלה . לבדורה . מן . זבח . ארץ .

(15) מצרים .

(1)   I, Ab Nishana, son of Sedaqa son of Jakob son of Sedaqa

(2)   son of Ab Chisda son of Obadiah of the family of Munes am writing

(3)   in Egypt. I wrote this Holy Torah for (..)

(4)   (..) (..) (..) (..) (..) (..) (..)

(5)   (..) (..) (..) (..) (..) (..) (..)

(6)   (..) (..) (..) Ab Romemata son of (..)

(7)   (..) (..) (..) (..) (..) (..)

(8)   Abraham son of (..) (..) (..) (..) (..)

(9)   Ab Romemata of the family of Iqara who paid

(10)   13 dinars of his own money. May Yahweh bless

(11)   it and may it instruct children and grandchildren. Amen.

(12)   In the year 878 of the reign of the sons of Ishmael (A.D. 1474)

(13)   And this completes the 18th Torah I have written.

(14)   Thanks be to God alone. Upon skins from the altar in the land of

(15)   Egypt.

On the surface it appears that there were three brothers, Aphiph, Ab Nis'ana and the present scribe, Ab Nishana, who produced a large number of manuscripts, eight of which are known to us. But underneath this assumption are several problems. Why would two brothers be given such similar names? Given the Samaritan tendency to freely exchange gutterals, they have essentially the same name. Is it really one person? If so, it is strange that he is inconsistent in the spelling of his own name, although not decisive. Neither von Gall nor Robertson record any manuscripts by Ab Nishana, but von Gall raises a question about the other two brothers: "Ist der Ab-Nis'ana identisch mit dem 'Aphiph . . . oder sind Ab-Nis'ana und 'Aphiph Bruder?" (1914-18: lxxxviii). Von Gall does not suggest why he thinks they may be identical.

Since my comparison of the handwriting of Aphiph (CW 2478a) and Ab Nishana (CW 2484) would not preclude the possibility that they are the same person, I asked the opinion of several qualified handwriting examiners supervised by Prof. C. H. Romig of the School of Criminal Justice. Two of the three examiners were of the unqualified opinion that both manuscripts were written by the same scribe. The third examiner had some reservations but generally agreed. Later I supplied them with a photocopy of a page from von Gall's gothic R. Four examiners compared the manuscripts, but were reluctant to draw any conclusions. Two of the four felt there were many similarities.

Common authorship would be compatible with

26

a chronological listing of the manuscripts of the three scribes correlated with the number of manuscripts the scribe claimed to have completed at that point. It would read:

1468/9	Ab Nis'ana	(Sassoon 403/ Ben-Zvi כח)	15th
1474	Ab Nishana	(CW 2484/ Ben-Zvi ל)	18th
1476/7	Aphiph	(von Gall I)	19th
1478	Ab Nishana	(Sassoon 404)	20th
1481	Aphiph	(Ben-Zvi לד)	28th
1482	Ab Nis'ana	(von Gall gothic R)	29th
1484	Aphiph	(CW 2478a)	31st
1485	Aphiph	(von Gall gothic P)	33rd

Circumstantial evidence strongly indicates a single copyist. The dilemma may be solved by supposing that Aphiph had a son, Nishana, providing Aphiph with the alternate name, Ab Nishana. A more likely hypothesis is that two of the three names are nicknames or honorific titles. The recipient of the manuscript is not known to us from any other manuscript.

Bills of Sale. The first of three bills of sale is found at the end of Genesis. It reads:

(1) אתעתקת . זאת . התורה . הקדושה . מן . [ממלכו . [

(2) פוחה . ברת . יקירה . ואקר . טוב . וקר ; [ורצלאה . [

(3) ועש ; וכת ; וסאם ; קהלה ; ואר ; קהלה . עש]ה . טבה [

(4) ואבי . אלמנה . ויתומה . ומסכינה . [אב . [

(5) רוממתה . בן . סהבה . טבה . ויקיר . וקמו] [

(6) ומסכינה . אברהם . בר . סהבה . טבה . וי] [

(7) קהלה . ומסכינה . אבי . רוממתה . דמב] [

(8) אל . ממלכת . יקירה . ואקר . טוב . וקר ; [ ]

(9) ועש ; וכת ; וסם ; קהלה ; ואר ; קהלה . ועשה . טובה .

(10) בדן . זבנה . יוסף . בר . סם ; קהלה . ואר ; קהלה .

(11) ומסכינה . עבד . העשר . בר . סם ; קהלה . ואר ; קהלה .

(12) ומסכינה . יוסף . דמבני . עבדה . בחמשה . עשר .

(13) דנארים . זהב . תהיה . בריכה . ומברכה . עליו .

(14) וילמד . בה . בנים . ובני . בנים . בעמל . משה .

(15) דמע . הנאמנים . בירח . שואל . שנת . אחד .

(16) ושמנים . ושמנה . מאות . שנה . לממלכת . ישמע ;

(17) אודיע . את . יהוה . וכתב . צדקה . בן . יושע . בן . הלוי .

(18) מתוחיה . בן . הצבי . בן . אברהם . בן . ברכה .

(19) דמן . קרית . הכהנים . שמש . המ ; הק ; י . יס ; יתה .

(20) מן . ארע . מצ ; בש ; אל . שכם . קר]ו[ב . אמן . בע ; משה . הנאתמן .

(1)   I transfer this Holy Torah from the possession of

(2)   Pu'a daughter of (..) (..) (..) (..) (..)

(3)   (..) (..) (..) (..) (..) (..) (..) (..)

(4)   (..) (..) (..) (..) Ab

(5)   Romemata son of (..) (..) (..) (..)

(6)   (..) Abraham son of (..) (..) (..)

(7)   (..) (..) Ab Romemata of the family of Iqara

(8)   unto the possession of (..) (..) (..) (..)

(9)   (..) (..) (..) (..) (..) (..) (..) (..)

(10)   (..) (..) Joseph son of (..) (..) (..) (..)

(11)   (..) Abd Ha^caschir son of (..) (..) (..) (..)

(12)   (..) Joseph of the family of Abada with fifteen

(13)   gold dinars. May it be a blessing and a blessing upon it

(14)   and may it instruct his children and his grandchildren.
       Through the merit of Moses the faithful.

(15)   In the month of Shawwal in the year

(16)   881 of the reign of the Ishmaelites (A.D. 1477).

(17)   I will make Yahweh known. Sedaqa son of Josua son of the Levite

(18)   Metuchiah son of Hassebi son of Abraham son of Beraka

(19)   who is from the city of the priests, the custodian, is the writer.
       May Yahweh in a short space of time restore in good the Holy Scroll

(20)   from Egypt unto Shechem. Amen. Through the merit of Moses the faithful.

Appropriately the seller is the daughter of the man who had the manuscript commissioned three years earlier. She may be the Pu'a who sold another Torah in A.H. 940 (A.D. 1523) and was at that time presumably the wife of Abraham of the family of Abada (Robertson 1962: 2). The new owner is not mentioned in another manuscript.

The witness is one of the most familiar figures in Samaritan bills of sale. His name ap-

pears in Sassoon 30 and 404, Ben-Zvi's ח (twice), ל (CW 2484), לז , von Gall's I, Y, ƒ (twice), n and Rylands II. He lived in Egypt and R. Gottheil infers that he held some office in connection with the Abischua scroll or copies made from it and preserved in Egypt (Gottheil 1906: 36).

The second bill of sale is found at the end of Exodus:

(1) [סמוך .] ממלכת . מן . הקדושה . התורה . זאת . אתעתקת

(2) ; קה . וסמוך . סהבה . בן . אברהם . קהלה . וארכון . קהלה

(3) . סהבה . בן . העשיר . עבד . ומסכינה ; קה . וארכון

(4) . ממלכת . אל . עבדה . דמבני . יוסף . ומסכינה . טבה

(5) ..טבה . סהבה . בן . יוסף . קהלה . וארכון . קהלה . סמוך

(6) . דמבני . צדקה . ממסכינה . טבה . סהבה . בן . אלה . עבד

(7) . מברכה . תהיה . דנר . עשר . שלשה . ומנחתה . רמח

(8) . אסיד . וכל . הגאמן . משה . בעמל . אמן . אמן . עליו

(9) וכתב . עבד . הטוב . בן . יעקב . בן . צדקה . דמבני .

(10) רמח . אודיע . את . יהוה . וכן . בחדש . גמדי .

(11) השני . שנת . שנים . ועשרים . ותשע . מאות .

(1)   This Holy Torah was transferred from the possession of (..)

(2)   (..) (..) (..) Abraham son of (..) (..) (..)

(3)   (..) (..) (..) Abd Ha^caschir son of (..)

(4)   (..) (..) Joseph of the family of Abada to the possession of

(5)   (..) (..) (..) (..) Joseph son of (..) (..)

(6)   Abdullah son of (..) (..) (..) Sedaqa of the family of

(7)   Remach and the price was 13 dinars. May there be a blessing

(8)   upon it. Amen. Amen. Through the merit of Moses the faithful.

(9)   Abd Hattob the son of Jakob son of Sedaqa of the family of

(10)   Remach witnessed and wrote this. I will make Yahweh known.

        Dated in the month of Jomada II

(11)   in the year 922 (A.D. 1517).

The seller is the brother of the buyer in the previous transaction. The buyer was involved in at least two other purchases. In A.D. 1511 he bought the manuscript designed יט and brought it to Shechem in A.D. 1520 (Ben-Zvi 1943b: 246). He also bought von Gall's gothic A in A.D. 1528 and sold it in 1554. Abd Hattob was the witness in the bill of sale in יט mentioned above, an undated bill of sale in Sassoon 403 and a bill of sale written in 1518 recorded in Ben-Zvi יד.

The last bill of sale in CW 2484 was written at the end of Leviticus and reads:

(1) קנה . זאת . התו . הקדו . חתנה . ט ; ריק ; וק ; רצ ;
ואקר . טוב . וחש ; וכ ; וסמ ;

(2) ק ; ואר ; צדקה . בן . סה ; ט ; ריק ; ואקר . טוב . וק ;
רצ ; וחש ; וכ ; ריק ; וסמ ; קה ;

(3) ואר ; קה ; ועשה . טב ; עבד . הטוב . בן . סה ; ט ; וס ;
ק ; וא ; ק ; ומסכינה .

(4) צדקה . דמבני . איקרה . מן . סה ; ט ; ויקי ; ואקר . טוב .
רק ; רצ ; רח ;

(5) ויד ; וס ; ק ; ואר ; ק ; וע ; טב ; יוסף . בן . סה ; ט ;
וס ; ק ; וא ; ק ; ומס ;

(6) עבד . רחמנה . דמבני . רמח . בדרך . הפקידות . ען .
רבתון . ברת .

(7) סה ; ט ; וס ; קה ; ואר ; קה ; ומסכינה . יוסף . בן . סה ;
ט ; ומס ; עבד .

(8) יהוה . דמבני . רמח [   ] מותו . ומן . אמה . פועה .
ברת . סה . ט ; ויק ;

(9) וס ; ק ; וא ; ק ; ומס ; אבי . הפתח . בן . ס ; וסמ ; ק ;
ומסך ; יהרה . דמבני .

(10) מתוחיה . מן . שכוני . דמשק ; במאה . אדומי . וכן .
בחדש . גמדי .

(11) האהד . שנת . א : וס : וט : מאות . לממשלת . בני .
ישראל . בסהדות .

(12) הסהדים . בו ; אודי . את . יה ;

(13) סהד . בכן . וכתבו .

(14) אברהם . בן . יוסף . בן .

(15) צדקה . הכהן . הלוי .

(16) סהד . במה . בן .

(17) וכתבו . אברהם .

(18) בן . צדקה . בן .

(19) הרבן . אית]מ[ר .

(20) שמש . המכ ; הק ;

(21) במצרים .

(1)   This Holy Torah was bought by (..) (..) (..) (..) (..) (..) (..)
(..) (..) (..)

(2)   (..) (..) Sedaqa son of (..) (..) (..) (..) (..) (..) (..) (..) (..)
(..) (..) (..)

(3)   (..) (..) (..) (..) Abd Hattob son of (..) (..) (..) (..) (..) (..) (..)

(4)   Sedaqa of the family of Iqara, from (...) (..) (..) (..) (..) (..) (..) (..)

(5)   (..) (..) (..) (..) (..) (..) (..) Joseph son of (..) (..) (..) (..) (..)
(..) (..)

(6)   Abd Rachmana of the family of Remach for the benefit of poor Rabbatun
daughter

(7)   of (..) (..) (..) (..) (..) (..) (..) Joseph son of (..) (..) (..) Obadiah

(8)   of the family of Remach [ ] after his death and that of her mother,
Pu'a, daughter of (..) (..) (..)

(9)   (..) (..) (..) (..) (..) Ab Happetach son of (..) (..) (..) (..) Jehora
of the family of

(10)   Metuchiah among the inhabitants of Damascus at a price of 100 edomites
and it is the month of Jomada I

(11)   in the year 961 of the reign of the Israelites (sic) (A.D. 1555) before

(12)   witnesses who will attest it. I will make Yahweh known.

(13-15)   Abraham son of Joseph son
of Sedaqa, the Levitical priest
is witness to this document.

(16-21)   Abraham son of Sedaqa son
of Rabbi Itamar
keeper of the Holy Writings in
Egypt
is witness to the content and text of this document.

The relationship of the seller to the rest of the Remach family is not clear. He may be acting as an agent for the two women or contributing a manuscript from his own collection. In A.H. 943 (A.D. 1536) he was the buyer of von Gall's gothic P. The buyer is possibly the same Sedaqa who sold Ben-Zvi's לד in A.H. 989 (A.D. 1582). The transaction was made for the sake of the orphan, Rabbatun.

The first witness, Abraham, also witnessed von Gall's I in A.H. 957 (A.D. 1550), gothic A in A.H. 961 (A.D. 1554), and U (no date). The second witness, Abraham the son of Sedaqa, was also a witness and buyer in the same bills of sale in I and gothic A and two bills of sale in von Gall's gothic P, one in A.H. 941 (A.D. 1534), the other in A.H. 943 (A.D. 1536). Another witness and some Arabic phrases are illegible.

Other Colophons and Additions. A rather long colophon on the last page explains that the repairs and rebinding were completed on the 5th day of the month of Rajab in the year A.H. 1303 (A.D. 1886) by Zebulun son of Isaak son of Joseph son of Ab Sekua son of Abd Chanunan son of Jakob son of Ab Sekua son of Abraham son of Ishmael son of Abraham son of Joseph son of Jakob son of Abdullah of the Danafite family.

The end of each **book** bears a record of the number of *qsym.*

Genesis	ספר . הראישון
250	קצים : ר ו ן c: -.:
Exodus	ספר . השני :-
200	קצים : ר . c: -c
Leviticus	ספר . השלישי -.:
136 in agreement	קצים : ק : ול : ון c: .:
with von Gall's I	
Numbers	ספר . הרביעי -.:
220	קצים : ר : וכ c: -.:
Deuteronomy	ספר . החמישי
160 in agreement	ק : וס : קצין :
with von Gall's H, N, P,	
gothic U, f, gothic O, h	

Underneath the previous colophon are two brief colophons separated by **a** design. The first reads:

תורה . תמימה
ברוך . נותינה

A completed Torah
Blessed be the giver.

There follows:

אן . הוה . הים . מלי . מן . מים . כן . כתבה . מלי
רחמים /.:
סחיוניך . סחירן /.: משקה . החיים
מגן . עדן /.:

As the sea is full of waters, so is scripture full of
compassion
May it cleanse you; a possession of life from
the garden of Eden.

CW 2481

Pentateuch
Samaritan, Aramaic and Arabic
Paper
739 pages
31.6 x 21.5 cm.
Text: 22.5 x 15 cm.
38 Lines
11 Letters per line per column
One Letter (Samaritan), Two Letter (Arabic)

Description. With its red leather cover
containing a tooled Arabesque design, CW 2481 is
the most attractive volume in the Chamberlain-
Warren collection. It is also impressive in
size. A flap extending from the back cover fits
over the front of the book. It is printed on
paper bearing incomplete water marks, ". . .
AZZUOLI," and "FF PAL . . .", a common paper in
Samaritan books of this period. A few pages also
bear a water mark of a triple crescent. A small
number of pages have patches, not very neatly
done.

When opened, each page is divided into
three columns, each defined by a double line in
purple ink. The text appears in three languages,
Samaritan Hebrew, Aramaic (a targum) and Arabic,
in that order, in columns from right to left.
There is no visible guideline for the scribe to
follow. The number of words in each Samaritan
paragraph is recorded in the margin and a cumula-
tive count of words appears at the bottom of each
page. A great variety of signs are used to di-
vide the larger sections of the Pentateuch. Most
of these involve various patterns of four "V"'s
with points facing each other. The sign at the
end of a *qsh* differs throughout both the Aramaic
and Hebrew.

According to a letter written from Barton
to Chamberlain on November 30, 1920, the manuscript had been bought for twenty pounds. During
its stay in the Three Oaks museum, it was on display and opened at the end of Exodus at which
point the two facing pages have been discolored
by exposure and dust. A note affixed to the page
reads: "Pentateuch read 460 times by Jacob Samaritan high priest." A series of notations in
Arabic on the back fly leaf represent Jacob's
recording of each of his readings of the text and
the total tallies with the Three Oaks note.
Jacob tells us in his own words why the text was
meaningful to him: "And after I finished (Sepher
ha-Yamim) I wrote a large Torah in two languages,
Samaritan and the Torah of the Jews, and I set
out the whole difference between them letter by
letter, paragraph by paragraph, word by word.
And I copied it from an old and perfect Torah
which has been in the synagogue for a thousand
years and compared it with the Torah of the Jews
which is in the *asshuri* (presumably Syriac?).
And it too is in my home at present" (Robertson
1962: 181). He claims it was written between
1879 and 1893.

Jakob's son, Abu'l Hassan, is quoted by
Barton (1921: 10) in reference to one of his
father's manuscripts, presumably CW 2481:

Now he had a Torah which comprised
three languages, viz. Samaritan Hebrew,
Syriac and Arabic, and he has persevered
in the copying of them for 13 years.
And the dire need forced him to offer
it for sale, and for the whole beautiful copy were paid the price of ten
paper Ottoman bank notes, value of each
paper 15 francs.

Date and Scribe. There are several colophons in the book and a major *tashqil.* The
latter is in the Hebrew (Samaritan) text only, as
opposed to the Murjan manuscript where the
tashqil appears in both the Arabic and the Samaritan. It begins on p. 613 and reads:

(1) אני . יעקב . בן . אהרן . בן . שלמה . כהנה . כתבתי

(2) הדה . המהותה . קדישתה . בשנת . שבעה . ותשעים

(3) ומאהים . ואלף . לממלכות . בני . ישמעאל . והיא

(4) מליו . יח . ארואן . אודה . את . יהוה

(1)   I am Jakob son of Ahron son of Schelama the priest.
         I wrote

(2)   this Holy Torah in the year 1297

(3)   of the reign of the sons of Ishmael (A.D. 1880) and it

(4)   completes the 18th Torah. I thank Yahweh.

Jakob was high priest from 1861 until the time of his death in 1916. Despite his personal poverty he provided very visible and worthy leadership for the community during that time. We are aware of an extensive literature that he produced as copyist, translator and author. He was in contact with several influential people including, William E. Barton, Moses Gaster and E. K. Warren. Dr. Gaster commissioned him to do several writings and record a census of the Samaritan community at Nablus (Robertson 1962: 275-83). Through his numerous colophons and letters he reveals considerable biographical information.

He was born in 1841, married in 1859 and had ten children, eight of whom preceded him in death. He supported himself to a great extent by selling printed copies of his essays. He had a long time feud with Isaac, son of the former high priest and later successor of Jakob. Some of the personal tragedies of Jakob's life are revealed in the colophons of CW 2481 as we shall see.

Colophons. At the end of Exodus Jakob wrote in A.H. 1310 (A.D. 1893):

(1) הוה . הכלולמן . מכתב

(2) תרגום . דן . ספרה . קדשה .

(3) ברמש . יום . חמישי . כג

(4) מן . חדש . השלישי . אשר

(5) אלחגה שנת . י . וגק . ואלף

(6) לממלכת . בני . ישמעאל

(7) על . יד . עבדה . מסקינה

(8) סגי . החטאות . יעקב . בן

(9) אהרן . בן . שלשה . בן . טביה

(10) כהנה : יסלח . לו . יהוה

(11) יכולה . ממנה . אמן

(12) אמן :. /

(1)   This completes the writing

(2)   of the Targum of this Holy Book

(3)   on Thursday evening the 23rd

(4)   of the third month which is

(5)   Al Haggah in the year 1310

(6)   of the reign of the sons of Ishmael
         (A.D. 1893)

(7)   by the hand of the miserable servant

(8)   fallen in sin, Jakob son of

(9)   Ahron son of Schelama son of Tabia

(10) the priest. Yahweh

(11) forgive him. Let it be an offering.
         Amen.

(12) Amen.

During the writing of Leviticus, misfortune befalls Jakob and he writes:

(1) הוה . הכלול . מן . מכתב . תרגום . דן . ספרה

(2) קדישה . ביום . החמישי . ז . מן . חדש

(3) הרביעי . אשר . הוא . מחרם . שנת . אחד

(4) עשר . ותלתה . מואן . ואלף . לממלכת

(5) בני . ישמעאל . ובעת . הוית . אכתב

(6) בזאת . התורה . אתה . עלי . יגונות

(7) ומחצות . רבות . ונכבדות . רבים . עד

(8) מאד . לא . אוכל . אספרם . מן . דן . התלנות

(9) אקמתי . במכתבה . שלשה . קשר . שנה

(10) כי . בראש . מכתבי . בה . מת . לי . בן . זכר

(11) ששים . יום ; ובתר . רפאותי . לקחתי

(12) ורבקשתי . אכלל . הוה . לי . בן . אהר

(13) ושמו . אהרן . בא . עליו . משפט . מרתה

(14) וטרפו . מן . קדשי . ובתר . מן . מחצתי

(15) מחצתי . ועזבתי . יתה . ארב[ד]

(16) שנים . עד . אן . אצלח . יהוה .

(17) יכה . עד . מאד . ושמו . יפה

(18) ובתרו . עזבתי . המכתב . בה

(19) תרי . שניה . וסבתי . יתה . בתר

(20) כן ודרשתי . אכתב . בה . רא . עלי.

(21) מחצ . ואדמתי . מכל . על . מדמוכי

(1)   This is the end of the writing of the Targum of this Holy Book

(2) on Thursday the 7th of the 4th month

(3) which is Muharram in the year

(4) 1311 of the reign of

(5) the sons of Ishmael (A.D. 1894) And during the time I wrote

(6-7) this Torah grief, a great wound and exceedingly great heaviness

(8) beyond measure fell upon me. Out of this calamity

(9) I stood three difficult years of writing

(10) because when I began to write my son Zachar died.

(11)   After 60 days I received some partial healing

(12) and I sought to finish it and then my next son,

(13) his name is Ahron (bring justice upon him) died

(14) and he was plucked from the saints and cut into my wound;

(15) my wound and the succour of pain lay in wait

(16) twice: When will I prosper O Yahweh?

34

(17)   It struck heavily again and his name is Japhet

(18)   and on his behalf I gave up writing in it

(19)   two years and I was surrounded by pain because of

(20)   this and I thought, I will still write in it.   My wound came upon me

(21)   and I became red from all my sorrow.

Jakob was to outlive eight of his ten children, three of whom died during this short period

indicated in the note. Two more notes are found
at the end of the book. The first reads:

(1)   הוה . הכלול . מן . מכתב . תרגום . זאת . התורה . הקדוש .
ברמש . יום

(2)   הששה . כח . מן . הדש . צפר . אשר . הוא . חדש . החמישי .
שנת . אהד

(3)   עשר . ושלש . מאות . ואלף . לממלכת . בני . ישמעאל . אשר .
היא . שנת

(4)   כז . וחמש . מאות . ושלשה . אלפים . למושב . בני . ישראל .
ארץ

(5)   כנען : על . יד . כתובו . העבד . המסכין . סגי . העונית .
והפשעות

(6)   והחטאות . יעקב . בן . אהרן . בן . שלמה . בן . טביה . בן .
יצחק

(7)   בן . אברהם . בן . יצחק . בן . צדקה . בן . טביה . בן .
אברהם . בן

(8)   יוסף : בן . טביה : בן . יוסף : בן . אברהם . בן . עבד .
אלה : בן . שלמה :

(9)   בן . בבא : בן . יצחק : בן . אברהם : בן . יצחק : בן . בבא .
בן . יצחק :

(10)   הכהן . הלוי . דמבני . קהת . נוף . אהרן . במדינת . שכם :
הקדושה :

(11)   אודת . את . יהוה . דכן . סעד . בחסדו . דרום . מן . אלה .
מן . רב .

(12)   טבהתו . וצדקתו . סליתות . חטאתו : בקדוש . תורותו : אן
על

(13)   דת . משה . ימיתו . ובעפר . הר . גרייזים . ישם . קברתו : ומן

(14)   בחורי . אחרית . ישם . אחריתו . ואן . לא . יצרכו . אל . אנש

(15)   כותו . ויצליח . דריכותו : וייטב . דבריתו : ועל . דת . משה

(16)   ימיתו : בעמל . התלתה : הזכאים . ויוסף . פתור . חלמותו :
ובעמל .

(17)   הנבי . דלא . קעם . ולא . יקום . קותו : אמן . אמן : ואקשתי
במכתב .

(18)   זאת . התורה . מן . שנת . ז . צ . ור . ואלף . אל . שנת . יא .
 וגק . ואלף

(19) מן . בב . המחצות . והתלנות . והיגונות . אשר . אתח . עלי

(20) מן . מות . ילידי . השלשה : וקוממות . השנאים . עלי : דלא . אוכל .

(21) אספר . צרותון . דשמו . עלי : מן . זה . אתרבת . עלי . עתיקות .

(22) דן . התורה : ולו . לא . סעדות . מרי . לא . יכלתי . על . כלולה . ועתקתי :

(23) תרגומה . מן : שלשה . תורות : והפרקן . בין . תרגום . ותרגום . שמתי . אתו

(24) על . כוסרי. זאת . התורה : אשול . מן . צדקת . כל . מן . קרא . בזה . התורה

(25) ידכר . כתובו . בטוב : ולא . ישכחני . מן . כקרת . הפתח : ואן . לא . יקרא .

(26) אדרשו . ביום . משינה . רבה ./.: / ושלום . יהוה . על . אדונן . משה . בן . עמרם . נדרש . תפלותו . ביום . נקם . ושלם /:

(1)   This completes the writing of the Targum of this Holy Torah on

(2) Friday evening the 28th of the month of Saphar which is the 5th month in the year

(3) 1331 of the reign of the sons of Ishmael (A.D. 1894) which is the year

(4) 3527 of the return of the children of Israel to the land of

(5) Canaan, by the hand of the writer, the unworthy servant who has fallen into sin and transgression

(6) and error: Jakob son of Ahron son of Shelama son of Tabia son of Isaak,

(7) son of Abraham, son of Isaak son of Sedaqa son of Tabia son of Abraham son of

(8) Joseph son of Tabia son of Joseph son of Abraham son of Abdullah son of Shelama

(9) son of Babaa son of Isaak son of Abraham son of Isaak son of Babaa son of Isaak

(10) the Levitical priest of the family Kohath Noph Ahron in the Holy City of Shechem.

(11)   I thank Yahweh in this witness of his mercy in the spirit of the God of strength for

(12) his goodness and righteousness and forgiveness of sin in his Holy Torah by the

(13) law of Moses who died and whose grave was placed in the dust of Mt. Gerizim. And from

(14) the time after they placed him no man shall have need

(15) and his way will prosper and his word will be good and upon the knowledge of Moses

(16) he will die; through the merit of the three pure ones and Joseph who interpreted his dreams and through the merit of

(17) the prophets who were slaughtered and did not give up hope. Amen.
Amen. And I labored hard in the writing of

(18) this Torah from the year 1297 (A.D. 1881) to the year 1311 (A.D. 1894)

(19) from the opening of the wounds and strife and grief which came upon me

(20) from the death of my three children. And a change came upon me as in
fasting

(21) I considered the distress which had come upon me in his name. I was
motivated to proceed with

(22) this Torah and I was not able to contain my bitterness, but I did not
stop when I finished it, but I went on to the

(23) Targum of the 3rd Torah making a division between Targum and Targum I
placed it

(24) upon the middle of this Torah. I require righteousness from all who are
named in this Torah.

(25) Let its writing be remembered for good and let me not be forgotten from
the beginning and whatever is not named.

(26) I seek the day of the great judgment. And now the peace of Yahweh be
upon the Lord Moses son of Amram. Let us seek his prayers in the day of
vengeance and peace.

Other Colophons and Additions. A last colophon, not written by Jakob, stands alone on the last
page. It reads:

(1) ‏זה . התורה . הקדושה . אשר . היא . מן . כיר .‏

(2) ‏אד . אדונן . הכהן . יעקב . בן . אהרן . אשר . הוא .‏

(3) ‏הכהן . הגדול . דהוה . בעתו . והוא . טרם .‏

(4) ‏מותו . בעשרים . יום . נתנה . אל . מסתר‏

(5) ‏וארן . מאהרה . בו . בדרך . המנחה :‏

(6) ‏וזה . הכהן . מת . ירחמו . יהוה . ומה‏

(7) ‏כתב . מנחתה . ואנחנו . נדע . כל . זה‏

(8) ‏על . כן . כתבנו . זה . הסהדה : הכתב . זה‏

(9) ‏בחדש . השני . שנת . ד . ול . וש . ואלף .: /. העד . במה .‏

(1) This Holy Torah which is from the hand of

(2) our lord the priest Jakob son of Ahron who is the

(3) high priest at this time and twenty days before

(4) his death he gave it to Mr.

(5) Warren as a gift.

(6) And this priest died, may God have mercy on him and the gift

(7) he wrote. We know all this

(8) therefore we write this witness which is written

(9) in the second month of the year 1334 (A.D. 1916).

Three witnesses attest the note:

(10) העד . במה . סופיר

(11) שלום . בן . אב

(12) סכוה . הדנפי

(13) בשכם .

(14) כתבו . זבולן

(15) בן . יצחק

(16) הדנפי : /

(17) סופיר . עבדה

(18) מסכינה . יצחק

(19) בן . עמרם

(20) הכהן

(21) בשכם

(10)   The witness to what is written is

(11) Shelama son of Ab

(12) Sekua the Danafite in

(13) Shechem.

The first book

250 *qsym*

And it contains

20,860 words

At the end of Exodus:

The second book

200 *qsym*

At the end of Leviticus:

The third book

135 *qsh*

At the end of Numbers:

The fourth book

218 *qsh*

At the end of Deuteronomy:

A complete Torah

"Blessed be the giver."

The fifth book

165 *qsh*

(14) Zebulon

(15) son of Isaak

(16) the Danafite wrote this.

(17) A witness to what is written is

(18) the miserable servant Isaak

(19) son of Amram

(20) priest

(21) in Shechem.

The colophon raises interesting questions. It is written by Jakob's life long enemy and successor. How and why did he gain access to the book if it had been given to Mr. Warren and why does he call it a gift after two other comments designated specific prices that were paid for it? Incidentally, this is one of the few references to Mr. Warren in the manuscripts.

Notes appear at the end of each of the biblical books in Arabic and Aramaic as well as Samaritan Hebrew. At the end of Genesis:

ספר . הראישון :

קצים . ר . ון : /.

ומלין . כ . אלף . וח

מואן . וס . מלה

ספר . השני : -

קצים . ר : -

ספר . השלישי :

קול . וה . קצה :

ספר . הרביעי .

ר . יח . קצה :

תורה . תמימה . ברוך .
נותינה .

ספר . החמישי .

ק . וס . וה . קצה .

38

All known Samaritan manuscripts record 250 *qsym* for Genesis; all but one agree on 200 for Exodus; a significant plurality (C E[1] H N P and the gothics U B F J O) support 135 against 134 or 136 for Leviticus; A B C E[1] N Q V support 218 in Numbers rather than 220 (G[2] H I P and the gothics U D E F J N O) and in Deuteronomy 165 is supported by A B C V against 160 in H N P and the gothics U F O (von Gall 1914-18: lxiii).

CW 2482

Pentateuch
Samaritan
Paper
489 Pages
10.9 x 9.7 cm.
Text: 6.5 x 3.5 cm.
36 Lines
19 Letters per Line
Two Letter

Description. In a letter from Dr. William Barton to Mr. F. W. Chamberlain dated November 30, 1920, he refers to a "dainty little Pentateuch for which I see Mr. Warren paid the equivalent of $25.00 to help a crippled tailor. It was a high price, but is a very pretty little book."

A note attached to the Pentateuch, presumably by the curator in Three Oaks, says that the tailor whose name was Tabir (sic: Tahor) Ibn Yakoub Sarawi bought a sewing machine with the case. "Tahor son of Yaqob, 27," is listed in the census commissioned by M. Gaster (Robertson 1962: 279) as "in the clothing trade, apprentice to a Gentile." He is of the family of Marhib.

The Pentateuch, on paper bound with green thread, has a tooled red leather cover and is neatly printed. The water mark is in a fancy script, but not enough shows to identify the company. "Extra Strong" is discernible in bold letters in the water mark. The size and the embellishments of the manuscript have the appearance of a novelty item. It is extremely small, containing 35-37 lines per page on a rectangle 6.5 x 3.5 cm. If a single word remains at the bottom of a *qsh* its letters are spaced out across the page. There are occasional terminal letters on a line written far to the left of the regular margin in the manner of several Arabic texts (Robertson 1938: 18, 24). The manuscript contains nine acrostics, including two in a circular form, and several notes.

Date and Scribe. The major acrostic begins with the א in ישראל in Num 8:18 and ends with the ה in יהוה in Num 14:16. It reads:

(1) אני . אב . הסדה . בן . יעקב . בן . אהרן . הכהן . כתבתי

(2) זאת . התורה . הקדשה . על . שם .] [טהור . בן .

(3) סהבה . טבה . ויקירה .] [הנסלה . על . רוחו . יעקב

(4) בישמעאל . הדנפי . תהיה . בריכה . ומברכה .

(5) עליו . אמן . וכן . בשנת . אלף . ושלש . מאת . ושלשם

(6) לממלמת . בני . ישמעאל . אודה . את . יהוה

(1)   I am Ab Chisda, son of Jakob son of Ahron the priest. I wrote

(2)   this Holy Torah on behalf of (   )   Tahor son of

(3)   (..) (..) (..) (   );   have mercy upon his soul, Jakob

(4)   son of Ishmael the Danafite; let there be a blessing

(5) upon it and a blessing upon him. Amen. It is the year 1330

(6) of the reign of the sons of Ishmael (A.D. 1912). I thank Yahweh.

Both the scribe and recipient are listed in the census that Gaster had done in A.D. 1884. Ab Chisda, son of Jakob, was 24 at the time of the census and is listed as a copyist. The index of volume II of Robertson's catalogue lists a wide variety of works including Pentateuch, liturgies and commentaries copied or translated from Arabic by Ab Chisda. Both Ben-Zvi (Ben-Zvi 1942a: 104) and Moses Gaster used Ab Chisda's services in compiling Samaritan materials. There are letters to Mr. Gaster from Ab Chisda in the Rylands collection (Robertson 1962: 267) reflecting some of his labors and some of his difficulties in dealing with Mr. Gaster. At the time of the present acrostic he would have been 52. The erasure was apparently made at the time of the writing of the note because the geneology that follows is appropriate for the recipient Tahor, who is also recorded in the census mentioned above. Tahor would have been 55 at the time this acrostic was written.

Other Acrostics. The other acrostics woven into the text are as follows:

(1) At Exod 2:2-2:10:

טוב . על . מה . אמה . אתילד . לגוה

A good woman and how I brought Moses forth a people.

(2) Contained within Exod 3:14-20:

יתרבי . זה . השם . הקדש

I will magnify this Holy Name.

(3) Contained in Exod 7:9-8:3:

ישתבח . עבוד . סימניה . ופליאתה

יממד . אתרבי . אלה . אלהים

I will praise the one who does signs and miracles; I will magnify the God of Gods.

(4) Contained within Exod 14:20-29:

יהוה . נצעיו . קרביה

Yahweh's help is near.

(5) Contained in a circular channel within Exod 31:1-11:

מי . ישמרה . אלה . ישמר

Whoever is watchful, God will watch over.

(6) Contained in Exod 34:1-7:

יהוה . אל . רחום . וחנון

Yahweh is a compassionate and gracious God.

(7) Contained in Lev 7:11-16:

חצי . התורה

Half of the Torah.

(8) Contained in Lev 26:3-13:

מברך . ורעעי . למן . שמר

A blessing and friendship to those who keep watch.

(9) Contained in Num 35:1-8 in a circular channel:

הר . גריזים

Mt. Gerizim.

Colophons. In addition to the acrostics, the author wrote a note upon the completion of each book of the Pentateuch. At the end of Genesis he wrote:

הוה . הכול . מן . מכתב . דן (1)

ספרה . בצפר . יום . חדה . יח (2)

מן . חדש . העשירי . שנת (3)

ל . וגק . לממלכות . בני (4)

ישמעאל : על . יד . כתובו (5)

עבדה . מסכינה . אב . חסדה (6)

בן . יעקב . בן . אהרן . הכהן : (7)

יסלה . לה . יהוה (8)

אמן : (9)

(10) ואקמתי . במכתב . דן . ספרה . תשע

(11) יומים . מלבד . יומי . השבתות :

(12) מודאה . לאלה . דכן . סעד .

(13) בחסדו .:

(1)   This completes the writing of this book

(2)   on Sunday morning the 18th

(3)   of the 10th month of the year

(4)   1330   of the reign of the children of the

(5)   Ishmaelites (A.D. 1912) by the hand of the scribe,

(6)   the miserable servant, Ab Chisda,

(7)   son of Jakob, son of Ahron the priest.

(8)   May Yahweh be merciful to him.

(9)   Amen.

(10)   And I was in the process of writing this book

(11)   9 days besides the Sabbath days.

(12)   Thanks be to God who gives support

(13)   in his mercy.

At the end of Exodus he wrote:

(1) הוה . הכלול . מן . מכתב . דן

(2) ספרה . קדישה . בערב . יום

(3) השני . כו . מן . חדש . ועשירי .

(4) והוא . מחרם . שנת . ל

(5) רגק . ואלף . לממלכת

(6) בני . ישמעאל . -:

(7) ומזדמן . אל

(8) ב . מן . חדש

(9) טיבת : על

(10) יד . עבד

(11) מסכי

(12) אב

(13) חסדה . בן . יעקב . בן . אהרן

(14) הכהן . יסלח . לו . יהוה . אמן

(1)   This completes the writing of

(2)   the Holy Book on Monday evening

(3)   the 26th of the 10th month

(4)   which is Muharram in the year

(5)   1330 of the reign of

(6)   the sons of Ishmael (A.D. 1912)

(7)   and corresponding to the

(8)   2nd of the month of

(9)   Tobit

(10)   by the hand of the

(11)   miserable servant,

(12)   Ab

(13)   Chisda son of Jakob son of Ahron

(14)   the priest. May Yahweh have mercy upon him. Amen.

At the end of Leviticus he wrote:

(1) הכלל . דן . ספרה . קדישה

(2) בצפר . יום . חדה . ג . מן

(3) חדש . אהד . עשר . והו

(4) צפר . המזדמן . אל

(5) ה . מן . טיבת . שנת

(6) ל . רגק . ואלף

(7) ישמעאל . יה :

(8) על . יד . כתו ;

(9) אב . חס ;

(10) בן . יע ;

(11) הכ ;

(1)   This Holy Book was completed

(2)   on Sunday morning, the 3rd of

(3)   the 11th month and it is

(4)   the morning corresponding to

(5)   the 5th of Tobit in the year

(6)   1331 of

(7)   the Ishmaelites (A.D. 1912).

(8)   By the hand of the scribe,

(9)   Ab Chisda

(10)   son of Jakob

(11)   the priest.

At the end of Numbers he wrote:

(1) הוה . הכלול . מן . מכתב . דן

(2) ספרה . קדישה . ביום . השני

(3) צהרים . יא . מן . חדש . אהד

(4) עשר . המזדמן . אל . יר . מן

(5) חדש . טיבת : שנת . ל . ורגק

(6) ואלף . לממלכת . ישמע ;

(7) על . יד . כתובו . אב

(8) חסדה . בן . יעקב

(9) בן . אהרן

(10) הכהן . יס ;

(11) לו . יה ;

(12) אמ

(13) ן

(1) This is the end of the writing of this

(2) Holy Book on Monday

(3) morning the 11th of the 11th month

(4) which corresponds to the 16th of the

(5) month of Tobit, in the year 1330

(6) of the reign of the Ishmaelites
    (A.D. 1912)

(7) by the hand of the scribe Ab

(8) Chisda son of Jakob

(9) son of Ahron

(10) the priest

(11) Yahweh forgive him.

(12-13) Amen.

And finally at the end of Deuteronomy:

(1) הוה . הכלול . מן . מכתב . זאת

(2) התורה . הקדושה . ביום . הרביעי

(3) מן . חדש . צפר . והוא . אחד

(4) עשר . המצדמן . אל . כה . מן . חדש

(5) טיבת . שנת . ל . ורגק . ואלף . לממל ;

(6) בני . ישמעאל . אשר . היא . שנת

(7) נ . והק . וג . אלף . למושב . בני

(8) ישראל . ארץ . כנען . על . יד . עבדה

(9) מסכינה . אף . חסדה . בן . יעקב

(10) בן . אהרן . בן . שלמה . בן . טביה

(11) הכהן . הלוי . יסלח . לו . יהוה

(12) אמן

(1)   This is the end of the writing of this

(2)   Holy Torah on Wednesday morning the

(3)   22nd of the month and it is the 11th month

(4)   which corresponds to the 25th of the month of

(5)   Tobit in the year 1330 of the reign of

(6)   the sons of Ishmael (A.D. 1912) which is the year

(7)   3514 of the return of the children of

(8)   Israel to the land of Canaan, by the hand of the

(9)   miserable servant Ab Chisda son of Jakob

(10)   son of Ahron son of Schelama son of Tabia

(11)   the Levitical priest. May Yahweh be merciful to him.

(12)   Amen.

42

The regular colophons at the end of the books read as follows:

ספר . הראש :
קצים . ר : רן :

The first book
250 *qsym*
.

ספר . השני .:
קצים . ר .: /.:

The second book
200 *qsym*
.

ספר . השלישי
ק ולה . קצה

The third book
135 *qsym*
.

ספר . הרביעי
ר ריח . קצה

The fourth book
218 *qsym*
.

ספר . החמישי
קצים ק וסא

The fifth book
161 *qsym*
.

CW 2483

Exodus
Samaritan
Paper
176 Pages
17.5 x 13.8 cm.
Text: 15.5 x 10.5 cm.
24 Lines
20 Letters per Line
Two Letter

This volume along with CW 10311, a copy of Leviticus by the same scribe, may belong to a set of Pentateuchal books. It is hand printed on a paper bearing no discernible water mark. The ink has faded to a brown hue. It is bound in a cover of purple cloth and leather and has a flap that can be drawn over the front edges of the book. Many patches, some of which are re- placements of whole pages are found throughout. On the new pages the water mark "SSB" and crescents are visible.

A brief colophon at the end of the book and a note pinned to the fly leaf with a common pin, both in Arabic, identify the text as a copy of Exodus written by Ghazal in A.D. 1749.

Ghazal, known also as Tabia, is one of the best known of the Levitical priests (Cowley 1905: 679). He composed many hymns found in various liturgical texts including a hymn on p. 267 of CW 2480 and p. 350 of CW 2486. He wrote commentaries and was the scribe of a wide variety of texts including liturgical, astro- nomical and scriptural writings.

In A.H. 1160 he hastily completed a service for the Dead to which he appended a note: "And the reader should not find fault with the writer since he copied it to the end with as much haste as possible in one day in the year A.H. 1160 (A.D. 1747).[22] Twenty years later he went to Gaza to find a wife and remained four years. Because of the depletion of the community there he came upon three Torah's (von Gall's gothic I, Ben- Zvi's לט and one other) which he bought and brought back to Shechem. He gave one of them to the synagogue in Shechem. He died six years later in A.D. 1786.

CW 10311

Leviticus
Samaritan
Paper
124 Pages
21 x 15.2 cm.
Text: 15 x 10.5 cm.
23 Lines
18 Letters per Line
Two Letter

The fact that this book and the previous book are in the same collection and are succeeding books of the Pentateuch could suggest that they are two of a five book set. However, the variance in size and binding and the four year gap between them suggests that Ghazal made more than one set and these are stray volumes from two different sets. The paper in these volumes, particularly the present one, is becoming brown and brittle. There are only two complete page replacements, but many patches occur throughout the book. The ink is an unfaded black. The old pages bear no water mark; "SSB" and crescents are found in the paper used for repairs. The cover is purple cloth with a light tan leather binding and edges. A rather lengthy ommission on p. 79 had to be corrected in the margin. Lev 18:28-30 on the same page has been carelessly circled in light pencil, perhaps accidentally or perhaps to underline the warning found there.

The colophon at the end of the book reads:

(1) כתב . זה . ספר . השלישי . בששת . ימים
(2) העבד . המסכין . הצריך . לוזמות
(3) יהוה . ורתותר: טביה . בן . יצחק
(4) בן . אברהם . בן . יצחק . בן . צדקה
(5) בן . טביה . בן . יוסף . בן . אברהם
(6) בן . טביה . הכהן . הלוי . יהוה
(7) יסלה . לו . חטאתו
(8) ויכפר . לו . אשמו
(9) אמן . בעמל . משה
(10) הנאמן . אמן :
(11) וכן . בשנ
(12) ת . ששה
(13) רשש
(14) ימ
(15) ומאה . ואלף . לממלכת . בני . ישמעאל . בחדש . צפר

(1)   I wrote this book of Leviticus in six days,
(2)   the miserable servant needing the mercy
(3)   of Yahweh and his grace, Tabia son of Isaak
(4)   son of Abraham son of Isaak son of Sedaqa
(5)   son of Tabia son of Joseph son of Abraham
(6)   son of Tabia the Levitical priest. Yahweh
(7)   forgive him his sins
(8)   and cover his guilt.

(9)   Amen. By the merit of Moses

(10)   the faithful. Amen.

(11)   And it is the year

(12-15) 1166 of the reign of the sons of Ishmael (A.D. 1753) in
         the month of Zophar.

The last line is under a patch, but the paper is sufficiently opaque to allow the text to be read. An acrostic, the usual, חצי התורה (Half of the Torah) is found on p. 24. At the end of the book surrounded by a pattern of "v"s and "c"s and dots and dashes is the notation:

ספר . השלישי

קצין : ק . ול : וד :

The third book
134 *qsym*

CW 10262

Pentateuch
Arabic
Paper
710 Pages
19 x 15.2 cm.
Text: 17 x 10 cm.
15 Lines
28 Letters per Line
Catchwords

Description. In its present condition with its cover falling off and the initial pages loose and frayed, the manuscript is in precarious shape, but is basically a handsome volume. The cover is red cloth with black bordered yellow stripes running vertically at about 2 cm. intervals. The binding is leather. The paper bears a water mark that is not clear. It appears each time as a segment of a circle in a corner of a page. Inside the circle are a cluster of small circles. The outer circle is double and seems to bear letters but they are not legible. The text is written in a black ink except for the titles done in red Samaritan majuscule characters at intervals of about ten pages. Some pages are missing toward the end of the manuscript and six leaves are missing from the beginning of the book of Leviticus.

Scribe and Date. At the end of Deuteronomy a brief note appears in Arabic: "By the hand of the most humble servant of God whose name is Shelama the son of Jakob the Damascene in the year 1685 A.D. on the 9th day of July." Shelama is not otherwise known. In the same year another manuscript, likely a sister to this one, was completed. The second manuscript is in the Bibliotheque Nationale in Paris.[1] The Paris copy, carrying the designation "Arabe 3", bears a note similar to the note following Solomon's (Shelama) colophon at the end of Deuteronomy. The note in CW 10262 reads:

This Holy Bible was copied from the old copy that was brought from Damascus from the house of its owner John the Damascene son of Qata. It was acquired and transferred to Paris by the Capuchin fathers in the year 1684 A.D. This complete and full size fine copy was written by the Samaritans and here are the various testimonies recorded at the beginning and end of it.

The last line refers to a series of notes produced below that are then copied in a fine hand similar to that in which the manuscript itself is written. The notes are copied from the same manuscript as the text.

Other Notes and Problems. Several problems arise. According to the text the last owner in Damascus was John son of Qata. According to a note in "Arabe 3" John (Yuhanna ibn Girgis ibn Qata of Damascus) was the scribe who finished "Arabe 3" in Paris in A.D. 1685 (f. 475v). A question of geography also arises. Both "Arabe 3" and CW 10262 agree that the model from which they have copied was brought to Paris by Capuchin priests ("rabbis") in 1684. Who then was the Samaritan who was in Paris to copy "Arabe 3" in the next year? Logically CW 10262 would also have been copied in Paris. How did it make its way back to Palestine and into the hands of Mr. Warren? Also what had happened to the model from which both of these have been copied?

A note at the top of the facing page in red ink reads:

Said, the servant of God who humbly begs the forgiveness and blessings of his merciful creator, the son of Sa^{c}ad al Basri, the Assyrian, may again the forgiveness of God be his. When I saw after reading the translation of this Holy Book with its unsound Arabic idiom which many claim was done by the venerable sheikh Abu Hassan the Syrian, may God have mercy on his soul, that this translation therefore could not be his. But it is the translation of the Jewish scholar al Fayoumi who truly erred in using the right Arabic idiom.

For this major reason I have found it necessary to discharge my obligation towards serving a good cause by translating this Holy Book from the Hebrew and Syrian languages into a more correct Arabic text with the hope that more copies will be done by future scribes. This will also replace the erroneous copy of al Fayoumi. Hoping that by thus doing I will, by the help of God secure for myself a good memory.

A cryptic note by another hand in black ink states that, "The sense of the above appears also on the second copy," perhaps referring to "Arabe 3" as the second copy.

The note may help tie together al Fayoumi, Abu-l-Hassan Suri and Abu Sa^{c}id in their relationship to the transmission of an Arab text of the Pentateuch. The note may be by Abu Sa^{c}id, a 13th century scribe whose name appears on Arabic translations of the Pentateuch. In the note he claims that the Arabic text he is familiar with is attributed to Abu-l-Hassan the 11th century scribe of the 10th century, al Fayoumi, also known as Sa^{c}adiah ben Joseph Gaon who did the first translation of the Old Testament from Hebrew into Arabic. It is characterized as a free translation, sometimes disregarding syntax or even paraphrasing whole chapters. It is apparently this looseness that disturbs Abu Sa^{c}id and prevents his attributing the text to Abu-l-Hassan.

The only other note in the front of the book is at the bottom of the facing page, at an angle from upper left to lower right. Since the lower left portion of the page is torn, much of this note is missing. It seems to record the marriage of a man named Shebaly in the year 1192 (A.D. 1778). It is the only note appended to this manuscript that is not a copy of a note from a previous model.

The rest of the notes are at the end of the book and are neatly copied from the original model. The first two notes, the brief note indicating the scribe and the next note describing the sojourn of the model from Damascus to Paris, are followed by several more in the following order:

(1) On Monday morning the 11th of Shaaban in the year 400 A.H. (A.D. 1010) the son of Ghanaim died. He was unique in his honesty. Written by the humble servant of God the son of Sedaqa the son of . . . A Sedaqa ibn Miha wrote one of the notes in "Arabe 3".

(2) On Monday night in the year 400 A.H. (A.D. 1010) the young man Ali Hassan Adi died. Alas for that beautiful face, wonderful personality and rich mind. We must submit to the will of our exalted God and humbly ask him to bestow his grace and sympathy on his saddened father, his brother and cousin Joseph (a Joseph ibn Sa^{c}id is another note writer in "Arabe 3").

(3) This is to testify that the lady of the house and her sister and the daughter of the late Sa^{c}adullah the son of Abraham the son of Sa^{c}adullah the Samaritan have on this date sold this Bible to the reverend sheikh the son of the late known sheikh the son of Fatthal the Samaritan for the known sum of two hundred and ten drachmas by the hand of Sedaqa the son of Joseph Hilly the auctioneer on the 12th of II Jomada in the year . . .

The three notes above are described as hav-

ing been at the end of the Book of Genesis in the original model. The following two notes were at the end of Deuteronomy:

(1) On this Holy Monday which is the last day of the month of II Rabia in 400 A.H. (A.D. 1010) Ann (Jan?) the daughter of our uncle the learned sheikh Joseph the son of the wise uncle Jakob has passed on to the graceful dwellings of the Lord God. It is the eve of the New Year. May God bless its days.

Said our master and lord, who holds the reign of the age, the forerunner of the present and who occupies the seat of succession of the noble family of Pinehas, who also astutely excels in the knowledge and interpretation of the Holy laws of Moses.

(2) On the blessed Sunday of the month of Jomada I the first of the year 400 A.H. (A.D. 1010) our aunt Staitah died. She was the daughter of our late uncle sheikh Abu'l Iz, the son of Abraham the son of Abu'l Iz the son of Ramih and the wife of uncle sheikh al-Assa'ad Sa'ad ad Deen the son of Shammer. She had four children, two daughters and two sons of whom one daughter and two sons were by uncle Sa'ad ad Deen and the other daughter by uncle Sa'adoun the son of Jakob the son of Sa'adoun. May God have mercy on her soul.

The following note, according to its superscription, was originally at the beginning of the model:

On the day of blessed Thursday the 15th day of II Jomada in the year 400 A.H. (A.D. 1010) the leading sheikh Ishmael the son of the pious uncle Sedaqa the son of the learned sheikh was blessed by a baby boy whom he named Joseph. Also on this day a baby boy was born to the learned sheikh Joseph the son of the late Rasheed which was given the name Sedaqa. May God bless the two newly borns with long and happy and pious lives. Amen. Amen. Amen. To the Lord of the universe written by the first worshippers of our exalted Lord. I testify that I am the humblest and neediest of all of his mercy and forgiveness. Jakob al Mutatuttib.

CW 2467, 10316, 10317, 10318, 10322

Pentateuch
Samaritan
Paper
Scroll
c. 147 Columns in 51 Sheets Sewn Together
Column: 15.2 x 30.4 cm.
Text: 14.4 x 24.8 cm.
60 Lines
40 Letters per Line

These five scrolls are practically identical and although hand printed seem to have been deliberately produced for sale to outsiders. Each is about 75 ft. long and bears a seal of the high priest attesting its authenticity. A Three Oaks museum note dates one of them (10322) in 1918. They all are done on paper bearing the "SSB" and crescent water mark. There are no notes or acrostics.

A typed note attached to one of the scrolls explains that the Samaritan community was so appreciative of Mr. Warren that they wanted to give him their famous Abischua scroll. When he refused it, so the note states, they gave him one of the paper scrolls. Since the note is no longer attached to any of the scrolls it is not clear which one was used in the display, but 2467 is attached to wooden rods with brass knobs and may be the "substitute." The source of the story is not indicated.

CW 11704

Part of Genesis
Samaritan, Aramaic, Arabic
Photo
21 x 18.5 cm.
Text: 19 x 16.5 cm.
51 Lines
c. 12 Letters per Line in Each of 3 Columns
Two Letter

There are two copies of each photo, one identical pair marked (a) and (b), the other (c) and (d). Both texts are in three columns in near majuscule with no vocalization marks. The pages are water stained and frayed. The pages were held flat by what appear to be metal strips nailed to a board with three nails. Photos (c) and (d) contain the text of Gen 2:4-15 beginning with אלה in Gen 2:4 and concluding with הלשמרה in Gen 2:15. Photos (a) and (b) contain the subsequent verses, Gen 2:16-25 beginning with אלהים in verse 16 and ending with יתבששות in verse 25.

CW 2468

Part of Genesis
Samaritan

48

Stiff White Cardboard
67 x 84.6 cm.
5 Columns per Sheet
80 Lines
25 Letters per Line per Column
Two Letter

These are very stiff pieces of cardboard rolled up together. The text is printed in neat modern uncials between margins that have been engraved into the cardboard. There are no notes or acrostics. The text runs from Gen 1:1 to 7:11 on the first sheet and 7:12 to 13:11 on the second sheet. Dividing designs composed of "c"s, dashes and dots are found in a horizontal line after Gen 3:24, 6:16 and 11:22. There is no indication how the sheets were to be used.

*CW 10320 (20 Volumes), 10309, 10314 and **Two** Other Volumes*

Each contains half of one book of the Pentateuch
Samaritan
Paper
16 x 11 cm.
21 Lines
15 Letters per Line
Text: 10 x 6.3 cm.

Description. This is a set of twenty-four volumes, each composed of half of a pentateuchal book handwritten on paper for the use of school children. Their usage is noted on a label in the Three Oaks museum notes and confirmed by the colophon in 26382 below. Each is simply done without decoration or *tashqil* and most include some notation at the end. With the exception of 26382 they were all done in A.D. 1915. They are bound in cloth-covered cardboard, usually brown, and each has an Arabic number on the cover. Neither the Arabic numbers, nor the Three Oaks number

seem to have a consistent rationale. The water mark "SSB" and crescents appear in each.

Genesis. Four of the volumes contain parts of Genesis. 26369 (162 pp., Gen 1:1-28:22, brown cover) has no colophon. The other three do. 26363 (176 pp., Gen 1-28, brown cover):

(1) הוה . הכלול . מן . מכתב . זה
(2) חצי . ספר . בראשית . הראש
(3) בצפר . יום . הרביעי . אשר
(4) הוא . ראש . התשיעי
(5) והו . מחרם . שנת . שלשה
(6) ושלשים . וגק . ואלף
(7) לממלכת . ישמעאל . על . יד
(8) כתובו . עמרם . בן . יצחק
(9) הכהן . יסלח . לו . יהוה
(10) אמן

(1)   This is the end of the writing of this
(2) first half of the book of Genesis
(3) on Wednesday morning.
(4) It is the first of the ninth (month)
(5) which is Muharram in the year
(6) 1330
(7) of the reign of the Ishmaelites (A.D. 1915) by the hand of
(8) its scribe, Amram son of Isaak
(9) the priest. May Yahweh be merciful to him.
(10) Amen.

Amram, who writes this and several of the subsequent texts is the son of Isaak son of Amram son of Shelama son of Tabia. He was born in 1889 and had at least one brother, Sedaqa, and two sisters, Miriam and Zahiya (Robertson 1962: 275). In one of the items listed in the Rylands catalogue he is listed as keeper of the Shechem synagogue and of the Great Name and the Holy Scroll (Robertson 1962: 76). Some days later he finished the second half of Genesis (26364, 140 pp. Gen 29-50, brown cover):

(1) הוה . הכלוה . מן . דן . ספרה
(2) בצפר . יום . השני . יב : מן
(3) חדש . התשיעי . והוא . עמנו
(4) מחרם . שנת . לג . רגק . ואלף
(5) לממלכות . בני . ישמעאל
(6) על . יד . כתובו . עבדה . מסכין
(7) עמרם . בן . יצחק . בן . עמרם
(8) בן . שלמה . בן . טביה . הכהן
(9) הלוי . יסלח . לו . יהוה
(10) אמן . אמן . אמן
(11) שלום . יהוה . על . הנבי . הצדקה
(12) התמים . הטהור . הנאמן . משה
(13) נדרש . תפלותו . ביום . נקם
(14) ושלם

(1) This is the end of this book
(2) on Monday morning the 12th of
(3) the ninth month and it is with us
(4) Muharram in the year 1333
(5) of the reign of the sons of the Ishmaelites (A.D. 1915)
(6) by the hand of its scribe, the miserable servant,
(7) Amram son of Isaak son of Amram
(8) son of Shelama son of Tabia the Levitical priest.
(9) May Yahweh be merciful to him.
(10) Amen. Amen. Amen
(11) The peace of Yahweh be upon the righteous
(12) perfect and good and faithful prophet Moses.
(13) Let us seek his prayers in the day of wrath
(14) and peace.

Another member of the family of Levitical priests, a cousin to Amram, who was also called a keeper of the Holy Places and the ancient

scroll, is the scribe of a second copy of the last half of Genesis. He is Tabia son of Pinechas son of Isaak son of Shelama son of Tabia. He was born in A.D. 1885 and had three brothers, Naji, a copyist, and Abraham and Maslih, who were priests. A number of materials in the John Rylands collection were copied by him. At the end of 26367 (137 pp., Gen 29-50, brown cover) he wrote:

(1) הוה . הכלול . מן . מכתב . זה
(2) ספר . בראשית . ביום
(3) הרביעי . בהמשה . עשר
(4) יום . מן . חדש . התשיע
(5) בשנת . אלף . ושלש . מאות
(6) [ושלש] . ושלשים . שנה
(7) לממלכת . בני . ישמעאל
(8) ראשול . מן . יהוה . אן
(9) תהיה . זאת . השנה
(10) א[ן]ר . ממלכותם . כי
(11) בזאת . גשנה . הוה
(12) מרחיבה . גדלה . בינם
(13) ובין . עדת . אלאנמריה
(14) ואני . עבדה . מסכינה
(15) טביה . בן . פינחס
(16) כהנה . ירחמו . יהוה
(17) וישכן . רוחו . בגן
(18) עדן . אמן . אמן

(1) This is the end of the writing of this
(2) book of Genesis on
(3) Wednesday the fifteenth
(4) day of the ninth month
(5) in the year
(6) 1330
(7) of the reign of the sons of Ishmael (A.D. 1915)
(8) I ask Yahweh how
(9) it will be in this year
(10) of their reign because
(11) in this Goshen there is

50

(12) great strife between them

(13) and the congregation of the faithful

(14) and I am the miserable servant

(15) Tabia son of Pinechas

(16) the priest. May Yahweh be merciful
    upon him

(17) and let his spirit dwell in the garden

(18) of Eden. Amen. Amen.

The last half of the note has overtones of
apocalypse. It is written out of distress al-
luded to in symbols intentionally avoiding the
mention of specific situations. The Samaritans
are in "Goshen," the biblical land of bondage
where they are oppressed by "them" and "their
reign," either the Ottoman Turks who have ruled
for four centuries or the British who are fight-
ing the Turks for control of the Levant. The
Samaritans are identified as the "congregation
of the faithful." Their distress will be more
explicitly spelled out in a later colophon in
the same series.

Exodus. There are five volumes containing
parts of Exodus. 26847 (116 pp., Exod 1-24,
brown cloth cover) has no colophon. The earliest
"first half of Exodus" volume containing a
colophon, 26361 (133 pp., Exod 1-24, brown cloth
cover), is by Amram:

(1) הוה . הכלול . מן . מכתב . חצי
(2) ספר . ואלה . שמות . בצפר
(3) יום . השלישי . כח . מן . חדש
(4) מחרם . שנת . לג . ושלש . מאות
(5) ואלף . לממלכת . ישמעאל . על . יד
(6) כתובו . המסכין . עמרם . בן
(7) יצחק . בן . עמרם . בן . שלמה
(8) בן . טביה . הכהן . הלוי . יסלח
(9) לו . יהוה . אמן . בעמל . משה
(10) הנאמן . אמן . :/

(1)   This is the end of the
       writing of half of

(2) the book of Exodus on

(3) Tuesday morning the 28th of the
    month of

(4) Muharram in the year 1333

(5) of the reign of the Ishmaelites
    (A.D. 1915) by the hand of

(6) its scribe the miserable Amram son

(7) of Isaak son of Amram son of Shelama

(8) son of Tabia the Levitical priest.

(9) May Yahweh forgive him. Amen.
    By the merit of Moses

(10) the faithful. Amen.

A week earlier he had completed a copy of
the second half of Exodus (26848, Exod 25-40,
brown cloth cover):

(1) הוה . הכלול . מן . מכתב . ספר . השני
(2) הקדוש . ביום . השלישי . כא
(3) מן . חדש . התשיעי . והו . מחרם
(4) שנת . לג . וגק . ואלף . לממלכת
(5) בני . ישמעאל . על . יד . כתובו
(6) עבדה . מסכינה . עמרם . בן
(7) יצחק . בן . עמרם . בן . שלמה
(8) בן . טביה . הכהן . הלוי
(9) יסלח . לו . יהוה . אמן
(10) בעמל . משה . הנאמן
(11) אמן . אמן
(12) אמן

(4) שנת . לג . ורגק . ואלף . לממלכת

(12) אמן

(1) This is the end of the writing of the second

(2) Holy Book on Tuesday the 21st

(3) of the ninth month which is Muharam

(4) in the year 1333 of the reign

(5) of the sons of Ishmael (A.D. 1915) by the hand of its scribe

(6) the miserable servant Amram son

(7) of Isaak son of Amram son of Shelama

(8) son of Tabia the Levitical priest.

(9) May Yahweh be merciful to him. Amen.

(10) Through the merit of Moses the faithful.

(11) Amen. Amen.

(12) Amen.

26848 may be intended as the second part of 26847 which bears no colophon.

The only book in this series specifically dated in a year other than 1333, and therefore presumably the earliest book in this series is 26382 (106 pp., Exod 25-40, brown cloth cover, a few corrections in red ink) begun by Amram and completed by Ab Chisda:

(1) חצי . זה . תמימות . הוה

(2) השני . ביום . הקדיש . הספר

(3) והוא . הראישון . חדש . מן . ד

(4) וגק . בל . שנת . הראש . גמאד

(5) ישמעאל . בני . לממלכת . ואלף

(6) עבדה . תמימותו . כתוב . יד . על

(7) יעקב . בן . חסדה . אב . מסכינה

(8) תממתי . ואני . הכהן . אהרן . בן

(9) עמרם . דדי . בן . כתובו . כי . אתר

(10) בומיץ . היה . הכהן . יצחק . בן

(11) לאלה . נשול . לכתב . יכל . ולא

(12) ברפאותן . ירפאו . המתרברב

(13) הנאמן . משה . בעמל . אמן . אמן

(14) אמן

(15) בני . נערי . שם . על . זה . ואכתב

(16) הנמצאים . השמרים . ישראל

(17) בעל . דפתהו . המדרש . בבית

(18) אלה : וארן . מסתר . הטובות

(19) וחיי . חייו . בימי . יאריך

(20) אמן . אמן . טוב . עמנו . מן . כל

(1) This is the completion of this half

(2) of the Holy Book on Monday

(3) the 4th day of the first month which is

(4) I Jomada in the year 1332

(5) of the reign of the sons of Ishmael (A.D. 1914)

(6) by the hand of the scribe who completed it

(7) the miserable servant Ab Chisda son of Jakob

(8) son of Ahron the priest and I completed

(9) it because its scribe, the son of my uncle, Amram

(10) son of Isaak the priest was ill

(11) and he was not able to write. Let us

(12) leave him to God, the Great and may he heal him in his sickness.

(13) Amen. Amen. By the merit of Moses the faithful

(14) Amen.

(15) And I wrote this on behalf of the children of the sons

(16) of Israel who keep the faith

(17) in the school house opened by

(18) the good Mr. Warren. May God

(19) prolong the days of his life and let

(20) all our days be good. Amen. Amen.

There are several points of human interest in this colophon. Ab Chisda takes up the task of completing the manuscript for the ailing Amram who is unable to write. Both are sons of priests and the two fathers have been involved in a bitter jealousy which the sons seem to have transcended. We also become aware of some of the direct aid that E. K. Warren gave to the Samaritans, in this case a school building for whose use these books were copied.

The last of the Exodus volumes was written by Tabia (26370, 101 pp., Exod 25-40, brown cloth cover):

(1) הוה . הכלול . מן . מכתבות . זה . ספר

(2) השני . בצפר . יום . הששי . בארבג

(3) ועשרים . יום . מן . חדש . מחרם

(4) אשר . הו . חדש . התשעי . שנת . אלף

(5) ושלש . מאות . ושלשה . ושלשים . לממלכת

(6) ישמעאל : על . יד . כתובו . דלביה . בן

(7) הנסלח . לו . פינחס . בן . הכהן

(8) יצחק . ירחמו . יהוה . וישכן

(9) רוחו . בגן . עדן . אמן . אמן

(1)   This is the end of the writing of this second book

(2) on Friday morning the

(3) 24th day of the month of Muharram

(4) which is the ninth month in the year

(5) 1333 of the reign of the

(6) Ishmaelites (A.D. 1915) by the hand of its scribe Tabia son of

(7) (may it be forgiven to him) Pinechas son of the priest

(8) Isaak. Yahweh have mercy upon him and may his spirit dwell

(9) in the garden of Eden. Amen. Amen.

The strange location of the expression "may it be forgiven him" implies some quarrel the scribe has had with his father, but there is no outside evidence and it may be a formal expression.

Leviticus. Three volumes all written in the same month and each containing a colophon incorporate parts of the book of Leviticus. The first is written by Tabia (26347, 84 pp., Lev 16-27, brown cloth cover):

(1) הוה . הכלול . מן . מכתבות . זה . ספר

(2) השלישי . בצפר . יום . הששי . באחד

(3) יום . מן . חדש . העשירי . בשנת

(4) אלף . ושלש . מאות . ושלשי . ושלשים

(5) לממלכת . ישמעאל . על . יד . עבדה

(6) מסכינה . שמש . בכנשת . שכם

(7) הקדושה . טביה . בן . הנסלח

(8) לו . פינחס . בן . אדונן
(9) הכהן . יצחק . ירחמון
(10) יהוה . וישכן . רוחון . בגן
(11) עדן . אמן . ונשול . מיהוה
(12) אן . יצילנו . מזאת . הימים
(13) ומעבדת . השנאים . אמן
(14) אהיה . אשר . אהיה . -:

(1) This completes the writing of this third book
(2) on Friday morning the first
(3) day of the 10th month in the year
(4) 1333
(5) of the reign of the Ishmaelites (A.D. 1915) by the hand of the
(6) miserable servant, custodian of the congregation at Holy Shechem,
(7) Tabia son of (may he be forgiven)
(8) Pinechas son of the Lord
(9) Priest Isaak. May Yahweh be merciful to him
(10) and let his spirit dwell in the garden
(11) of Eden. Amen. Let us ask Yahweh
(12) when he will deliver us from these days
(13) and from the servant of hate. Amen.
(14) I will be who I will be.

Here is another reflection of the misery of the community brought on by the First World War. Amram is the scribe of the other two volumes of Leviticus. At the conclusion of the first (26359, Lev 1-15, 80 pages, brown cloth cover) he writes:

(1) הוה . הכלול . מן . מכתב . זה
(2) חצי . ספר . ויקרא . בצפר
(3) ירם . הששי . ב . מן . חדש
(4) העשירי . והו . עמנו . צפר
(5) שנת . לג . ורגק . ואלף . לממלכת
(6) בני . ישמעאל . על . יד . כתובו
(7) עמרם . בן . יצחק . בן . עמרם
(8) בן . שלמה . בן . טביה . הכהן
(9) הלוי . יסלח . לו . יהוה . כל
(10) עון . ופשע . וחטא . ושגג
(11) בעמל . משה . הנאמן . אמן
(12) אמן . אמן

(1) This completes the writing of this
(2) half of the book of Leviticus on
(3) Friday morning the second day of the
(4) 10th month which is with us, Saphar,
(5) in the year 1333 of the reign
(6) of the sons of Ishmael (A.D. 1915) by the hand of its writer,
(7) Amram son of Isaak son of Amram
(8) son of Shelama son of Tabia the Levitical priest.
(9) May Yahweh forgive him all
(10) sin and transgression and trespass and error.
(11) By the merit of Moses the faithful. Amen.
(12) Amen. Amen.

At the conclusion of the other (26366, Lev 16-27, 64 p., brown cloth cover) he wrote:

54

(1) הוה . הכלול . מן . מכתב . ספר

(2) ויקרא . בצפר . יום . השלישי

(3) גי . מן . חדש . צפר . שנת

(4) לג . וגק . ואלף . לממלכת

(5) בני . ישמעאל . על . יד

(6) עמרם . בן . יצחק . בן . עמרן

(7) יסלח . לו . יהוה . אמן

(8) בעמל . משה . הנאמן . אמן . :./

(1)   This completes the writing of
       the book

(2)   of Leviticus on Tuesday morning

(3)   the 12th day of the month of Saphar
       in the year

(4)   1333 of the reign

(5)   of the sons of Ishmael (A.D. 1915)
       by the hand

(6)   of Amram son of Isaak son of Amram

(7)   May Yahweh be merciful to him. Amen.

(8)   By the merit of Moses the faithful.
       Amen.

Numbers. The same two scribes are responsible for from four to six volumes containing parts of the book of Numbers. The ambiguity arises from two volumes (26849, Num 1-15, 106 pp., red cloth cover and 26371, Num 1-15, 108 pp., brown cloth cover) which bear no colophons, and another (26383, Num 16-36, 130 pp., purple cloth cover) whose scribe is not mentioned in the brief colophon:

(1) הוה . הכלול. מן . מכתב . זה

(2) הספר . בצפר . יום . החמשי . יג . מן

(3) חדש . השני

(1)   This completes the writing of this

(2)   book on Thursday morning the 23rd of

(3)   the second month.

The earliest dated colophon in a copy of Numbers (26356, Num 16-36, 127 pp., brown cloth cover) reads:

(1) כללתי . דן . ספרה . ברמש . יום׳

(2) החמישי . בחמשה . עשר . יום

(3) מן . חדש . צפר . שנת . אלף . ושלש

(4) מאות . ושלשה . ושלשים . שנה

(5) לממלכת . בני . ישמעאל . ואני

(6) עבדה . מסכינה . שמש . בכנשת

(7) שכם . הקדושה . טביה . בן

(8) פינחס .כהנה . ירחמו

(9) יהוה . וישכן . רוחו . בגן

(10) עדן . אמן . אמן . אמן

(1)   I finished this book on
       Thursday evening

(2)   on the 15th day

(3)   of the month of Saphar in the year

(4)   1333

(5)   of the reign of the sons of Ishmael
       (A.D. 1915) and I

(6)   am the miserable servant,
       custodian of the congregation

(7)   at Holy Shechem, Tabia son of

(8)   Pinechas the priest. May Yahweh
       be merciful to him

(9)   and let his spirit dwell in the garden

(10)   of Eden. Amen. Amen. Amen.

Here Tabia leaves out the expression, "May he be forgiven," before his father's name. 26362 (Num 1-15, 96 pp., brown cloth cover) bears the colophon:

(1) הוה . הכלול . מן . מכתב . זה . חצי
(2) ספר . במדבר . סיני . בצפר . יום
(3) חמישי . כב . מן . חדש . צפר
(4) והוא . עמנו . העשירי . שנת
(5) לג . ורגק . ואלף . לממלכת
(6) ישמעאל . אשר . היא . שנת . סב
(7) והק . רג . ואלף . למושב . בני
(8) ישראל . ארץ . כנען . על . יד
(9) כתובו . עמרם . בן . יצחק . בן
(10) עמרם . בן . שלמה . בן . טביה
(11) הכהן . יסלח . לו . יהוה . אמן
(12) בגמל . משה . הנאמן . אמן
(13) אמן . אמן
(14) אמן

(1) This completes the writing of this half of
(2) the book of Numbers on
(3) Thursday morning the 22nd of the month of Saphar
(4) which is with us the 10th (month) in the year
(5) 1333 of the reign
(6) of the Ishmaelites (A.D. 1915) which is the year
(7) 3562 of the return of the sons of
(8) Israel to the land of Canaan, by the hand
(9) of its writer Amram son of Isaak son of
(10) Amram son of Shelama son of Tabia
(11) the priest. May Yahweh be merciful to him. Amen.
(12) By the merit of Moses the faithful. Amen.
(13) Amen. Amen.
(14) Amen.

The colophon in the remaining Numbers volume (26360), Num 16-36, 113 pp., brown cloth cover) reads:

(1) הוה . הכלול . מן . מכתב . זה
(2) חצי . ספר . במדבר . סיני

(3) בצפר . יום . השני . כה . מן
(4) חדש . צפר . שנת . אלף . ושלש
(5) מאות . ושלשה . ושלשים
(6) שנה . לממלכת . ישמעאל
(7) על . יד . המסכין . עמרם . בן
(8) יצחק . בן . עמרם . בן
(9) שלמה . הכהן . יסלח . לו
(10) יהוה . כל . עונו . ופשעו
(11) וסדר . אשמו . בעמל . בן . עמרם
(12) רבנו . שלום . יהוה . עליו
(13) ועל . אבותיו . ואראשיו
(14) אמן . אמן
(15) אמן

(1) This completes the writing of this
(2) half of the book of Numbers
(3) on Monday morning the 25th of
(4) the month of Saphar in the year
(5) 1333
(6) of the reign of the Ishmaelites (A.D. 1915)
(7) by the hand of the miserable Amram son of
(8) Isaak son of Amram son of
(9) Shelama the priest, may Yahweh forgive him
(10) all his sins and transgressions
(11) and take care of his wrong doings. By the merit of the son
(12) of Amram our teacher. The peace of Yahweh be upon him
(13) and upon his fathers and his fiancee.
(14) Amen. Amen.
(15) Amen.

Deuteronomy. Amram does two of the volumes of Deuteronomy, one bears no colophon (26348, Deut 1-17, 98 pp., brown cloth cover), but the most interesting colophon of the series is written by Jakob in his lone contribution (26421, Deut 16: 18-34, 83 00., red cloth cover):

(1) הוה . הכלול . מן . מכתב . זאת

(2) התורה . הקדושה . בצפר . יום

(3) השלישי . כח . מן . חדש

(4) מחרם . והוא . ראש . חדש . התשעי

(5) שנת . לג . ורגק . ואלף . למשלות

(6) ישמעאל : אשר . היא . שנת

(7) ג . ס . והק . ורג . אלף . לממשלת

(8) ישראל . על . יד . עבדה . מסכנה

(9) סגי . החטאות . והפשעות

(10) יעקב . בן . אהרן . בן . שלשה . בן

(11) טביה . הכהן . הלוי . יסלח

(12) לו . יהוה . בעמל . משה . הנאמן

(13) אמן . ומן . יום . אחלתי . במכתב

(14) זאת . התורה . ומטרם . שני

(15) הדשים. ועד . כללתי . זאת

(16) התורה : והצרר . מתרברב . עלינו

(17) בגלל . המלחמה . אשר . קדמת . בין

(18) אלדולה . אלעסמליה . ואלאלמאניה

(19) ואלנמס[]יש . ובין . דולה . ברטאניה

(20) ומסקוף . ואפראנסה : ודולה . אלעס

(21) אספר . כל . אשר . ממצא . בין . אנשי

(22) דולתהא . ולקחו . ובזזו . כל

(23) מצאו . מן . קמח . ושערה . וגפן

(24) ותצנה . ושמן . ודבש . ושכר

(25) ובגדים . וכלים . מן . נחשת

(26) וברזל . ומן . הכסף . והזהב

(27) ומן . הצאן . והבקר . וגמלים

(28) וסוסים . וחמורים . רב . ען

(29) מותן . לא . נוכל . על . מספרן

(1)   This completes the writing of this

(2)   Holy Torah on Tuesday morning

(3)   the 28th of the month

(4)   of Muharram and it is the first of the ninth month

(5)   in the year 1333 of the rule

(6)   of Ishmael (A.D. 1915) which is the year

(7)   3563 of the rule of

(8)   Israel, by the hand of the miserable servant

(9)   fallen in transgression and sin

(10) Jakob son of Ahron son of Shelama son of

(11) Tabia the Levitical priest.
     May Yahweh have mercy on him.

(12) By the merit of Moses the faithful.

(13) Amen. And from the day I started writing

(14) this Torah two months ago

(15) and until I finished this

(16) Torah great suffering has come upon us

(17) on account of the war which arose between

(18) the armies of the Arabs and Germans

(19) and Austrians and the armies of British

(20) and Russia and France and the armies of the Turks.

(21) They conscripted all whom they could find among men

(22) of the army and they took and plundered

(23) all they could find of meal and barley and vines

(24) and (?) and oil and honey and alcohol

(25) and clothes and everything made of coppe

(26) and iron and of silver and gold

(27) and from the sheep and cows and camels

(28) and horses and donkeys in such great

(29) number that it is impossible to count.

The already impoverished people were apparently plundered by the Turkish army which also conscripted their young men. According to one source, 24 men, one fourth of the male populatio was drafted (Barton 1921: 4). This was a seriou threat to the existence of the community. They were also concerned about the demeaning of their religiously based pacifism and the coercion to shave their heads. Four died in the war and three were missing as of March, 1919. The community sold many of its belongings, including manuscripts, to raise money to bribe Turkish authorities to release or exempt their men. I find no indication of the success of this effort

The other two volumes of Deuteronomy were written by Amram and bear almost identical colophons. 26358 (Deut 1-16:17, 86 pp., brown cloth cover):

(1) הוה . הכלול . מן . מכתב . חצי
(2) דן . כתבה . ברמש . יום
(3) הרביעי . כז . מן . חדש . צפר
(4) שנת . לג . ושלשה . מאות
(5) ואלף . לממלכת . בני . ישמעאל
(6) הצריך . אל . רחמות . יהוה
(7) עבדה . עמרם . בן . יצחק
(8) בן . עמרם . בן . שלמה . בן . טביה
(9) הכהן . הלוי . יסלח . לו
(10) יהוה . אמן . בעמל . משה
(11) הנאמן . אמן . אמן . אמן

(1)   This completes the writing of half
(2)   of this scripture on Wednesday evening
(3)   the 27th of the month of Saphar
(4)   in the year 1333
(5)   of the reign of the sons of Ishmael
      (A.D. 1915)
(6)   by one who is needy of the mercy of
      Yahweh,
(7)   the servant Amram son of Isaak
(8)   son of Amram son of Shelama son of Tabia
(9)   the Levitical priest. May Yahweh
      forgive him.
(10) Amen. Through the merit of Moses
(11) the faithful. Amen. Amen. Amen.

and (26365 Deut 16:18-34, 90 pp., brown cloth cover):

(1) הוה . הכלול . מן . ספר . אלה
(2) הדברים . בצפר . יום . השני
(3) ג . יום . מן . חדש . רביע
(4) הראש . שנת . אלף . ושלש
(5) מאות . ושלשה . שלשים
(6) שנה . לממלכת . ישמעאל
(7) על . יד . כתובו . המסכין
(8) עמרם . בן . יצחק . בן . עמרם
(9) בן . שלשה . בן . טביה . הכהן

(10) הלוי . יסלח . לו . יהוה
(11) כל . עולו . ופשעו . ואשמו
(12) אמן . בעמל . משה . הנאמן
(13) אמן . אמן . אמן

(1)   This is the completion of the book
       of Deuteronomy
(2)   on Monday morning
(3)   the 3rd day of the month of I Rabia
(4)   in the year
(5)   1333
(6)   of the reign of Ishmael (A.D. 1915)
(7)   by the hand of its scribe the miserable
(8)   Amram son of Isaak son of Amram
(9)   son of Shelama son of Tabia the
       Levitical priest.
(10)   May Yahweh forgive him
(11)   all his sins and his transgressions
       and his trespasses.
(12)   Amen. Through the merit of Moses the
       faithful.
(13)   Amen. Amen. Amen.

The Marble Inscription: CW 2472

Samaritan Inscriptions. On top of one of the cartons of Samaritan materials in the Chamberlain-Warren collection was a rectangular piece of stone with an inscription in quite squared characters. After deciphering the first two lines I made a rubbing of the inscription and sent it to Professor James Purvis at Boston University who recognized it as the first inscription in the article by Professor Strugnell (1967: 555-80).

The inscription is one of four found at Emmaus (Strugnell 1967: 556), a village 20 miles from Jerusalem on the road to Joppa. The first was discovered in 1881 by Clermont-Ganneau inscribed into an Ionic looking capital (1882: 22-27). It reads:

ברוך שם ועולם

Blessed be the name forever.

The other two inscriptions were both found by Fr. M. J. Lagrange. The so-called 3rd inscription reads:

ופסח יהוה על הפתה
ולא יתן חמשית לבא

Yahweh will pass over the door and will not allow the destroyer to enter. (Exod 12:13) (de Vogue 1896: 433-34)

The other inscription, referred to as the second (Lagrange 1883: 114-16), is of particular interest because it is an exact parallel to the Chamberlain-Warren inscription. Both begin with Exod 15:3 and both conclude with a verse affirming the uniqueness of Yahweh, either rhetorically, "Who is like you," as in the Chamberlain-Warren inscription or explicitly, "None is like you," as in the second Emmaus inscription. The second Emmaus inscription reads in full:

יהוה גיבור במלחמה יהוה
שמו יהוה נחיתו
בא ברוך יהוה
אין כאל ישרון

Yahweh is a hero in war. Yahweh
is his name. Yahweh you have led it.
Come blessed of Yahweh;
There is none like the God of Jeshurun.

Two later Samaritan inscriptions from Damascus (Sobernheim I and Musil IV) also contain Exod 15:3. The paucity of Samaritan inscriptions greatly limits the generalizations that can be made about them.

CW 2472

Exod 15:3 and 11
Samaritan
Marble
31.0 x 12.2 x 5.0 cm.
3 Lines
Incised Horizontal Guidelines
Larger Half Broken Off and Missing

Description. The piece is of white marble with dark blue strains. A sizeable portion of the face of the inscription bears a reddish

stain. A cross section looked at from the end is
trapezoidal in shape with the long side bearing
the inscription. Only the ends and back are
unfinished, suggesting that the top and bottom,
as well as the inscription face, were exposed.
The back has been deeply scratched and pieces of
mortar still cling to the crevices. The end on
which the inscription begins, the right end
facing the inscription, carries the stump of what
may have been a key to hold the piece in place
against the wall of a building. Slightly more
than half of the inscription is missing, so there
is no clue as to the nature of that end.

The inscription reads:

יהוה גיבור בה [מחמה יהוה שמו]
מי כמוך באיל[ים יהוה מיכמוך]
נדרי בקדש נורא [תהלת עשה פלאה]

> Yahweh is a hero in [battle; Yahweh
> is his name]
> Who is like thee among the god[s, O
> Yahweh, who is like thee?]
> Majestic in Holiness, terrifying
> [in glorious deeds]

Brackets enclose the lost portion of the text.
It is composed of two verses, 3 and 11, from the
15th chapter of Exodus. Four words differ from
renderings in the standard Hebrew or Masoretic
text. גיבור (warrior) replaces the explicitly
anthropomorphic איש (man) in line one; the inscription has the variants כמוך for כמכה and
באילים for באלם in the second line and
נדרי for נאדר in the last line. Each new
reading has support in other Samaritan inscriptions or manuscripts.

A problem does arise at the point of the
break in line one. Following the Masoretic text
and all known Samaritan texts, the next letter
should be a מ. However, the marks left on this

inscription would not accomodate a מ and Professor Strugnell has appropriately proposed a ה
which could be accommodated. Although the noun
may be used with the definite article ה, there
is no such usage found in the Bible in combination with the prefix ב, nor is there any support for this reading in known Samaritan manuscripts.

Date. The critical question with all Samaritan inscriptions is the dating. Only the El
Ma inscription, a limestone piece inscribed with
the Decalogue found in 1935, offers a verifiable
date. It has been dated to the third century
A.D. on the basis of archeological evidence provided by the building of which it was a part.
Starting from there a rather general chronological hierarchy has been set up (Purvis: 1968).
The first and third Emmaus inscriptions are
thought to be the earliest available and date
probably in the first century A.D., although
W. R. Taylor dates them before the Christian era
(1941: 5). The El Ma inscription is pretty well
established as belonging in the third century.
The remaining inscriptions are held to the time
between the El Ma inscription and the destruction
of the Samaritan communities during the first
half of the sixth century.

The major evidence for dating the present
inscription is paleographical, through a comparison of the letters of this text with those that
have been more closely dated. This method was
used very successfully by John Trevor in dating
the first Dead Sea Scroll finds where he could
compare them with several distinctive and well
dated texts. It is much more difficult with
Samaritan texts because the Samaritans intentionally perpetuated an archaic form of Hebrew
characters and the distinctions between various
periods are often quite subtle. The only other
indications of date are the lack of punctuation,

word dividers or spacing between words, all characteristic of earlier inscriptions.

There are thirteen letters in the present inscription. ב and ש look pretty much the same in all the inscriptions. The ו is closest to the early Emmaus inscriptions. The ד and ח are very similar to the El Ma inscription of the third century. The remaining letters are closer to later inscriptions with the כ and מ having the latest forms. This means that the present inscription is either quite eclectic or that the texts are not as standard as we might wish. If the present chronological model is correct, it is most likely that the Chamberlain-Warren inscription dates between the third and sixth centuries A.D. In any case it demonstrates the difficulty of dating Samaritan inscriptions at this time. Unfortunately, manuscripts which are more easily dated either by colophons or chemical tests when necessary, are not available from this early period. Inscriptions are still too sparse and with the exception of the El Ma inscription, impossible to date other than by paleographical evidence. The present inscription cannot be dated with precision, nor can it at this point contribute to the dating of other inscriptions, but it is one more piece in a very complicated chronological puzzle and one that in the long run brings us closer to a resolution of the problem.

Content. The biblical chapter from which these lines are taken is one of the finest examples of Hebrew literary effort. It is the Song of Moses, a magnificent poem expressing the joy of release from bondage, vindictive bitterness toward the former oppressor and affirmation and confidence in the God who made the escape possible. This chapter of Exodus and the Decalogue or ten commandments constitute the most popular source of Samaritan inscriptions. The importance of the Decalogue is self evident. The signifi-

cance of the 15th chapter of Exodus is not so explicitly evident, but it is not incomprehensible. In terms of power and imagery, it is a fine piece of literature and is very likely among the earliest as well as finest Hebrew writings we have. Part of the chapter surely comes from a later time since it describes events from the period following the exile as if they had already occurred. But the first eleven lines and the Song of Miriam are probably contemporary with the events they describe, encapsulating the depth of feeling of the most profound event in Israel's life.

The present inscription circumscribes both beginning and end of that earliest poem; that is, it includes the first and last verses, 3 and 11. Verses 1 and 2 serve as prologue. Whether this is coincidental, sensitive selectivity or vestigial awareness of the original compass of the poem would be helpful for our understanding of the text and of the Samaritans.

It should also be noted that this chapter climaxes and concludes the biblical account of the escape from Egypt. Some Old Testament scholars contend that the first 15 chapters of the book of Exodus, or at least the latter parts of it, constitute a liturgical text that was read at certain festive occasions to unite subsequent generations around a common historical tradition. In any case, whether as the climax of a liturgical text, the boundaries of an early poem or key verses of a fine piece of literature, the choice of this text is not inexplicable.

Reasons for the choice of these lines can also be found in the life of the Samaritan community. The Samaritans were a community continuously harassed and persecuted, by the Jews from the very beginning, then along with the Jews under Antiochus IV, Pompey and particularly Hadrian, and most severely by the Christians in the three centuries they ruled Palestine. Justinian practically annihilated the Samaritan community in the first half of the sixth century A.D. The early Muslim period provided a moment of relief, but with the advent of the Ottoman Turks, the Samaritan community was again severely repressed.

Communities in such circumstances are left with few options. They can flee and many Samaritans did. They had their own *diaspora*: a fine brass scroll case crafted by one of the Samaritans in exile in Damascus and at least one Pentateuch written by an exile in Cairo. If members of a persecuted community choose to remain, they can stand their ground and face martyrdom; many thousands of Samaritans experienced this fate through the centuries. They can also remain and submit to the oppression of their masters. In such cases men usually dream of supernatural salvation or very natural vengeance. The former often takes the shape of apocalyptic vision while the latter is usually expressed in messianic terms, the expectation of a military leader to restore freedom to the community. The two visions are sometimes blended.

The Samaritan community recognized only the Pentateuch as canonical scripture and therefore had no apocalyptic or messianic heritage with which to work. Frustration in this bondage had to find expression within the limits of five books that contained no vision of the future. But they did present a view of the past and a moment in the past reflecting the Samaritan's own condition and hopes, a moment of bondage and deliverance. The Samaritans experienced all the bitterness reflected toward Egypt in the Song of Moses and longed for the joys of a new Exodus. And their hope was in the same God who had led the Israelites out of Egypt, a God strong in battle who would even the score. "Who is like this God among all Gods?" The author of the second Emmaus inscription is too impatient with rhetorical questions and hastens to affirm, "There is none like the God of Jeshrun!" Both

inscriptions speak from canonized scrpture to the heart of the hopes of the community.

Use of the Inscription. Samaritan inscriptions found *in situ* have been located either in the walls or lintels of homes or synagogues. The quality of stone and workmanship of the Chamberlain-Warren inscription would favor the likelihood of a synagogue. The length of the original piece would be somewhat longer than two feet, raising the possibility that it could be a lintel over a door or located above or below a window. This location would perhaps also better account for the shape and finish of the stone. If it were simply inlaid in a wall it would require neither a trapezoidal shape nor a finished top and bottom. As a lintel piece standing between two posts, more imaginative use of display could be employed. The word of God, the only real strength of the community, was thus thrust before all potential enemies as warning and safeguard.

The Brass Scroll Case: CW 2465

Scroll Case
Brass with Inlaid Silver Design and Samaritan
    Inscription
51 cm. high
Ca. 19 cm. diameter

While reading the introduction in von Gall's work I first became aware that this case was probably in East Lansing. He described a scroll case that had been purchased in ". . . 1905 (by) E. K. Warren in Three Oaks, Michigan." I immediately called the University Museum, for no such item had been in the boxes I was shown, and the scroll case was located. It is an impressive and attractive work. Three horizontal sections are hinged together, so they may be laid out flat or folded together into a cylinder completely enclosing any scroll placed inside. Each section has a third of the top and bottom attached to it so that the closed case protects the scroll on every side. The metal from which the case was cut was originally a single piece of brass upon which some craftsman had cut a design presumably intended for a tray. It contains Arabesque designs and Muslim religious slogans in Arabic. It is not obvious to me why the tray was abandoned and the metal used to shape a scroll case. It does seem strange that the Samaritans were not bothered by the fact that the inner lining of a case they built to house their most sacred possession contains Muslim religious phrases.

Each external panel of the case is divided into two sections each containing a 7.3 cm. silver inlaid Arabesque design. A border surrounds the entire panel and also divides the two sections. The border contains a series of inlaid inscriptions that have been published both in von Gall (1914-18: lii), and also in an article on this scroll case written by Hans Spoer in 1906 (105-07). When the case stands upright and open, the central band dividing each panel into two sections bears the inscription:

יברכך . יהוה . וישמרך

Yahweh bless and keep you.

Each section bears one of the three Samaritan words. On the six horizontal borders is written in order:

ויהי . בנסע .
הארון . ויאמר .
משה . קומה .
יהוה . ויפוצו .
איביך . וינוסו .
משנאיך . מפניך .

When the ark departed, Moses said, "Rise Yahweh, scatter your enemies and cause those who hate you to flee from before you."

The craftsman has written his own note around the top and bottom borders of the case:

(Top of case) (1) בשם . יה . עשה . זה . הארון . למכתב
(2) הקדוש . בדמשק . העבד . המסכין . נשיש
(3) בוראי . אלה . אבי . הפתח . בן . יוסף . בן
(Bottom) (4) יעקב . בן . צפר . דמבני . מנשה . יה . יכפר
(5) חטאתו . אמן . בשנת . שלשים . ותשע . מאות
(6) לממלכות . בני . ישמעאל . על . יד . יצחק . ה . . .

In the name of Yah(weh). I made this case for the Holy Writing in Damascus. (I am) the miserable servant, the least of the creatures of God, Abu'l Fath son of Joseph son of Jakob son of Zophar of the family of Manasseh. Yahweh forgive his sins. Amen. In the year 930 of the reign of the sons of Ishmael (A.D. 1524) by the hand of Isaak . . . .

Neither the craftsman nor Isaak, whose role is not clear, are otherwise known.

One last inscription appears inlaid in the lower section of the middle panel:

64

. כתבו . פינחס
. בן . אלעזר .

Written by Pinechas son of Eleazar

Presumably this is the Pinechas who was high priest from 1508 until 1548 when he died. In 1523 he fled to Damascus (Ben-Zvi 1943a: 416) where a year later he inscribed this case. In 1526 he wrote a note in Ben-Zvi's יח, "Blessed be the Lord by whose Holy Grace I will return to Shechem." But it was eleven years before he was able to return to Shechem (1538).

The journey of the scroll case from the time of its making until its arrival in Three Oaks is not well attested. It may have been brought to Shechem by Pinechas and may have thereafter housed the Abischua scroll in Shechem. Von Gall believes it did. In 1860 the Abischua scroll was transferred to its present case "from an old brass case" (Barton 1921: 18). There is no evidence regarding its location from that time until it passed into the hands of E. K. Warren. Even that transaction is not clear. The note attached to the case in the Three Oaks museum says that it was a gift from Jakob in 1913. Spoer, writing in 1906, identifies it as the property of Mr. Warren so the later date cannot be right. James Purvis describes the purchase of the scroll by Mr. Warren from Jakob with the help of Mr. Fareed of the American Colony and a travel agent named R. Floyd and says there were unpleasant incidents experienced by both sides in the transaction (Purvis 1972: n.30). Presumably this transaction took place in 1905.

MARKAH

Markah: CW 26349

Teaching of Markah
Samaritan and Arabic
Paper
681 pp.
23.5 x 16 cm.
Text: 15.7 x 11 cm.
26 Lines
26 Letters per Line

Introduction. John MacDonald in his compre-
hensive work on *Memar Markah* characterizes the
work as "a thesaurus of early Samaritan traditions, hymns, beliefs, saws and epithets . . . ."
MacDonald 1963: xviii). There are six books
within the work. The first begins with Moses'
experience with the burning bush and continues
through the Red Sea victory. The second deals
with God's part in the deliverance of Israel,
with particular attention to an interpretation of
Exod 15. The third book discusses the responsi-
bilities of the Israelite leaders and people.
The fourth book is strictly theological. The
fifth treats the death, ascension and subsequent
glorification of Moses. The last section returns
to theology and a mystical treatment of several
Hebrew letters.

Markah was the son of Amram son of Sered and
according to later tradition, a high priest.
MacDonald (1963: xx) and Cowley's (1909: xxi)
speculation on alternate forms of Markah's name
(Marcus, sometimes טיטס Titus) and his son Nanah
(Nonus) lead them to assume that Markah lived
while Syria had a Roman government and he is usually dated somewhere in the period from the 2nd
to 4th century A.D. Markah is the most highly
venerated of all non-biblical personages by the
Samaritans.

MacDonald assumes two main types of fixed
texts of Markah: those copied by the Danafite
family and those written by the Levite family.
The former is a superior text, more likely to
follow the original reading. MacDonald is aware
of three Levitical manuscripts of Markah:

(1) 938 (A.D. 1532) by Shelama son
    of Amram son of Shelama and
    Abraham son of Pinechas son of
    Isaak son of Solomon.
(2) 1227 (A.D. 1812) by Solomon son
    of Sarur son of Joseph son of
    Sarur son of Joseph son of Sarur
    son of Isaak
(3) 1283 (A.D. 1870) by Ab Chisda
    son of Jakob son of Aaron son
    of Solomon.

CW 26349 is a Levitical text that would fall according to date between (1) and (2) above. Mac-
Donald characterizes the Levitical texts as having ". . . a multitude of variant spellings and
inconsistencies of orthography and a substantial
number of unimportant additions. They Hebraize
forms much more than the Danafite manuscripts and
usually agree together on synonyms against the
Danafite manuscripts (1963: xxxi).

Description of CW 26349. The above description of the Levitical texts is very apt for
26349. The volume itself is done quite neatly in
two columns, Samaritan on the right, Arabic in
Samaritan characters on the left. In poetic
sections the first word of each line often stands
alone on a line in large majuscule. A few designs occur, for example between the word "doer"

66

and "of miracles" as a description of God on p. 72. Every tenth page is numbered in majuscule Samaritan characters at the top of the page with a series of three dots at top, bottom and sides of the number. A page of notes on the back fly leaf seems to be missing. The work is bound in red cloth with brown leather binding.

Date and Scribe. Several dated notes in Arabic are found throughout the text. None indicates when the work was begun, but otherwise the notes keep us informed of the progress during the writing and events for some time afterward. In chronological order the notes are:

(1) P. 129: Ghazal ibn Isaak ibn Ibrahim ibn Isaak ibn Sadaqa ibn Ghazal, the Levite priest finished this volume on Tuesday the 7th of II Rebia corresponding to the 14th of Athur which is Hatmin Hophni 1163 (A.D. 1750). The second volume follows.

This marks the completion of the first of the six books by Ghazal, who was also the scribe of CW 2483 and CW 10311, where biographical material is discussed.

(2) P. 389: He started (this book) on Friday the 11th of I Jomada 1163 (A.D. 1750).

(3) P. 537: On Friday 17th of II Jomada 1163 (A.D. 1750) Ghazal the son of Isaak the Levite priest finished this part. (A prayer has been written beside the note.)

(4) P. 674: This 'Teachings of Markah' was finished Sunday morning the 14th of Shaban corresponding to the 14th of Hozaran 1165 (A.D. 1752) by Ghazal son of Isaak son of

Ibrahim son of Isaak son of Sadaqa son of Ghazal the Levite priest, guardian of Shechem. God bless him and all his descendents and make his way easy in everything.

There is no note to indicate when the work was begun but the completion of the first section was in 1750 and the total volume is completed, according to this note, two years later.

Other Colophons.

(1) P. 538: On Sunday, which is not blessed because on the 28th of I Jomada 1166 (A.D. 1753) the Levitical priest Ibn Ibrahim died while the writer was in Gaza with Abu Sarur who is called Ghazal al Matarri. They sent a messenger for us and the messenger told us. We immediately returned to Nablus where we arrived on Thursday the 2nd of II Jomada corresponding to the second month 1166 (A.D. 1753). Then on the night of fasting on Mt. Gerizim they elected a priest in his place. God bless him. The writer is Ghazal ibn Isaak ibn Ibrahim.

During the year following the completion o the text the book is still in the possession of the scribe. While on a trip to Gaza with his brother-in-law Abu Sarur, he learns of the death of the high priest, his uncle, Ibn Ibrahim and within four days of the death he has returned to Nablus. The reason for the urgency of his return is that he is the likely successor. Ghazal is elected to fill the vacancy.

(2) P. 675: On Friday afternoon on the
1st of Muhurram, 1195 (A.D. 1781)
God gave to לה כתיה Amram, God
bless him, through the prophet
Amram. Peace be upon him. And on
Saturday the 2nd of Muhurram, 1195
(A.D. 1781) (he gave) to our brother
Ismail son of our uncle Jakob who is
nicknamed Kabib el Danfi, a boy and
he named him Isaak, God bless him
through Ibrahim and Isaak. It is
written by Ghazal son of Isaak
the priest.

Here Ghazal records two births. The first
is likely his own son, Amram. The other is a
child born to a friend in the Danafite family.
Ismail is mentioned in only one other instance as
the recipient of a Pentateuch (Rylands II) as a
gift from his Aunt in 1782.

(3) P. 677: Friday evening the 19th of
II Rebia corresponding to the 10th
of Athar 1197 (A.D. 1783) the writer
of the book was presented with a boy
who was named Salama. Peace be upon
him and may God make him live a long
life.

When Salama grew up he wrote beside
this note another: Salama ibn
Ghazal, keeper of peace and definer
of wisdom read these Holy Teachings
carefully and he wrote this note in
Shaban corresponding to I Kanun
1216 (A.D. 1802).

The first note announces the birth of
Ghazal's only other known child. Succeeding it
is a note written 19 years later by Salama himself. Salama's name appears frequently as a
scribe of parts of liturgical texts (Cowley L 9,

A.D. 1838; L 12, A.D. 1811 and L 21, A.D. 1845),
a hymn writer (Rylands item 337 A) and the buyer
of a Pentateuch (von Gall's V, A.D. 1799). Items
XXIII and XXIV in the Rylands collection also
refer to him as a teacher of a "Hebrew astronom-
ical science." Rylands codex IV records an inci-
dent when Salama became high priest and there was
a difference of opinion whether they should celebrate Passover. Salama prevailed and the Samaritans went up on Mt. Gerizim to celebrate, but
had to pitch their tents on rocky ground because
the rest of the area was under cultivation.

(4) P. 388: Abdul son of the writer
Ghazal looked into this Holy Book
in 1224 A.H. (A.D. 1809).

This implies a third son beside Amram and
Salama unless Abdul is a nickname.

(5) P. 389: Isaak son of Salama son of
Ghazal son of Isaak son of Ibrahim
looked into this book on the 7th of
Ramadan corresponding to the month
of Kanun 1250 (A.D. 1834) and the
winter that year was very cold.

We are now down to the second generation,
the grandson of the scribe of this volume.
Isaak, the grandson, is known as a scribe of some
parts of Rylands 30 in 1830 in which he records
an eclipse of the moon that lasted two thirds of
the night and caused much outcry. He also wrote
a number of hymns (Rylands items IX, XII, XIX,
94, 97, 102, 122, 127, 162, 368).

(6) P. 680: (Two notes appear. The
first is undated.) This Holy
Teaching was appended by Isaak son
of Salama son of Isaak son of
Ibrahim. (The second) On the
appendix of this Holy Teaching

which was spoken by our lord Markah, Sunday in the month of Ayar 1250 A.H. (A.D. 1835), I am his slave Isaak son of Salama son of Ghazal son of Isaak son of Ibrahim son of Sadaqa son of Ghazal son of Joseph son of Ibrahim son of Ghazal the priest. This book was read by the governor of Syria, Ibrahim Paasha, God make the people use this book.

These are two notes regarding an addition made by Isaak, the writer of the previous note. He reports that the governor of Syria read the book. Ibrahim was Paasha of Syria from 1831-1840. It would be interesting to know the occasion of his meeting with the Samaritans.

(7) P. 539: Salih son of Ibrahim son of Salih son of Murgan the Danafite looked into these Holy Prayers which were said by Markah our master. God bless him. 29th I Jomada, 1263 (A.D. 1847).

Salih, a distant relative of the family that owns the book is well known for his work as a copyist of several of the Rylands items. In 185 he requested that the high priest Amram unroll the Abischua scroll so that the *tashqil* could be read. It was unrolled and a dittographed word was scraped off (Robertson 1938: 233-34).

LITURGICAL TEXTS

Samaritan Liturgies

More than one hundred liturgical manu-scripts appear in catalogues of various Samaritan collections. They cover a wide range of festi-vals (Sabbaths, Passover, Unleavened Bread--sep-arated from Passover by the Samaritans--Weeks, Booths and Atonement) and special occasions such as circumcision, marriage and burials. Generally they are written in a cursive hand with occasion-al responses and significant letters of acrostics in majuscule. Scriptural portions are in contin-uous paragraph form or small triangular patterns, the latter containing only the beginning of the verse and concluding with "etc." in Arabic. The hymns are usually in two columns of doubled lines. Instructions to the congregation or leader are often in double lines alternating in color (par-ticularly red and black) and utilizing varying amounts of Arabic. Usually, if not always, there are catchwords, that is, the first word of each left hand page appears at the bottom of the right hand page.

There are several common elements that fre-quently occur. A new service usually begins with some form of "In the name of Yahweh . . ." often followed by a title like "the Merciful," or "the Victorious." The name of the Service is then given (for example, "Service for the Sabbath of Unleavened Bread.") The service consists of various poems, scripture readings, hymns and re-sponses, many of which are so well known to the congregation that only the first few words are indicated in the book. Some parts are given special names. A "Markah" and a "Durran" are common. The former represents a poem attributed to Markah, the latter represents short works pre-sumably by Markah's father Amram Durah (hence "Durran") son of Sared. Another specific element of the service is the *qataf*, a sort of free as-sociation linking of scriptural passages suggest-ed by a shared word.

Sections of the service are often divided by a short liturgical statement, usually in majus-cule, such as "I will be what I will be," "There is no God except the One," and "God is Great." Occasionally a service calls for a series of pro-strations accompanied by appropriate prayers.

The largest part of the service is taken up with hymns or poems of various length. Most characteristic of the shorter poems are those that begin with חילה "power" or בגדלו "in his greatness." There are more than fifty of each. Two of the most popular are:

בגדלו . בחרך . אה . ישראל

In His Greatness He chose you O Israel.

חילה . דבחר . אדם

Out of His power He chose a man.

Within the Chamberlain-Warren collection the first appears in 2480, p. 2; 2486, p. 13; 10313, p. 96; 26344, p. 98; the latter in 2480, p. 239; 10313, p. 1 and 26344, p. 97.

The longer poems are likely to be acrostics, each stanza beginning with a subsequent letter of the alphabet. The gutterals ע, ח, ה, and א are often exchanged in the acrostic as elsewhere in Samaritan writing. Stanzas are in double columns of four lines each. A popular example, composed by Markah, begins:

אתחו . אלהנן : ואלה . אהתך

You are our God and the God of our fathers.

Among the Chamberlain-Warren manuscripts it appears in 2480, p. 93; 2486, p. 133; 26344, p. 23 and 26343, p. 96. There are also a number of acrostics in which the first letter of each line or stanza will spell out the name of the author.

These various liturgical elements are brought together in rather consistent patterns interspersed with instructions in poor Arabic to form the liturgies. There are six examples of liturgical works in the Chamberlain-Warren collection.

CW 2480

Passover Prayers
Samaritan with Arabic Instructions
Paper
389 pp.
22.5 x 16 cm.
Text: 10 x 14 cm.
Catchwords

Description. CW 2480 is a book of prayers and services for Passover. It is bound with white, green and red thread into twenty fascicles, protected by a red leather envelope style cover with a flap extending over the front. A design has been tooled into the leather of the cover. The pages bear a water mark consisting of some combination of the capital letters "FF PALAZZUOLI", sometimes accompanied by three crescents. The writing is generally minuscule.

Most of the text is in black ink. Green ink is used sparingly, most obviously for optional texts that may be added or omitted in the service. Purple and later orange ink is used frequently for several functions: rendering of alternative readings in a service, instructions, contrasting color in alternative verses, responses and important words.

There are many decorations within the text. Colophons are often set off in boxes or teardrop shaped patterns or zigzag lines carrying dots. At several points in the text (pp. 74-76, 143, 144, 147, 159, 160, 161, 213, 226, 271, 272, 327-329) biblical verses are started in the form of triangles and the triangles alternate in color. When the scribe has written all the words that will fit in the triangle, he writes "and so forth" in Arabic.

P. 83 contains a half page (lengthwise) illustration of the site of sacrifice on Mt. Gerizim. Two purple circles about 4 cm. in diameter and about 8 cm. apart are joined by a corridor 1 cm. wide. The lines forming these shapes are all tripled. The circle at the top of the page is shaded and represents north where the people who will make the sacrifice stand. The bottom circle represents the altar and the corridor is where the boiling water is prepared.

Other unique decorations are a pair of linked rosettes on p. 84 and a circle 5 cm. in diameter on p. 128. The latter is formed by leaving a blank space 1 cm. wide through the text.

Several acrostics identifying hymn writers are found throughout the text, usually using letters at the beginning of the line which are indicated by underlining or the use of different colored ink: p. 3-4 Tabia, 187 Abu Aziz, 189 Markah, 203 Tabia, 222 Tabia, 252 Isaak (in red letters randomly selected throughout the text), 268 Pinehas.

In three instances congregational responses are abbreviated by use of the first letter of each word:

P. 148 ff.

ה ; י ; א ; ב ; י ; מ ; מ ; ע ; צ :

הוציא . יהוה . את . בני . ישראל . מארץ . מצרים . על . צבאתה

Yahweh brought forth the children of Israel from the land of Egypt against armies.

P. 333

ו ; א ; ה ; ה ; ל ; מ ; י

ושמרת . את . החקה . הזאת . למועדה . מים . ימימה

And you shall keep these statues at the appointed time every day.

P. 369 ff.

ק ; צ ; מ ; א ; ר

קבל . צלותן . מנן . אה . רחמנה :

Receive a portion of our wealth, O compassionate One.

During its stay in the Three Oaks museum the book was opened to pp. 143-44 which are gray with dust.

Scribe and Date. The scribe is Ragib son of Jakob son of Ishmael son of Abraham of the Dana-fite family. He tells us of his progress four times in the course of the codex as the following notes will indicate. According to an Arabic note on p. 373 it was completed on Sunday noon the 10th of Rebia in A.H. 1307 (October, A.D. 1890). The scribe is not otherwise known to us:

I finished writing this Holy Service which contains the service of Passover, the evening of the feast and the feast and the service of the Seven Days, morning and evening, with the help of God and his grace on Sunday noon the 10th of I Rebia 1307 A.H. corresponding to 22nd Tishri I, 1306 corresponding to the Samaritan calendar's eighth month by the poor man seeking God's forgiveness, Ragib son of Jakob son of Ishmael son of Ibrahim the writer, the Israelite, the follower of Moses. God forgive him and forgive

his relatives and those who taught him and all the people of Israel who worship at Mt. Gerizim in the House of God.

I give this blessed prayer book to my brother who is the son of my mother and my father; I hope that God will bless this gift and bless our male descendents who inherit the book. I hope he is going to read this to correct the errors in writing and grammar. I pray that God will bring success to all who correct any mistakes.

Content. This book, like several other liturgical texts, is divided into twelve parts:

I. Morning of the first Sabbath of the first month (p. 1ff).
II. Noon (p. 8ff).
III. Evening (p. 13ff).
IV. Second Sabbath morning (p. 23ff).
V. Noon (p. 29ff).

VI.   Passover Night (p. 41ff).

VII. Prayers for the evening of the Feast of
      Passover (p. 56ff).

VIII. Morning of Passover (p. 85ff).

IX.   Schedule of work for the Day of Passover
      (p. 159ff).

X.   Service for the Feast of Passover
      (p. 219ff).

XI.   Sabbath of Unleavened Bread (p. 239ff).

XII. Evening of the Last month, the Memorial
      Sabbath (p. 247ff).

Hymn Writers. The hymn writers cited by name in this volume are:

Abd Allah son of Barakh al Hiftawi, 265

Abd Allah son of Ibrahim al Hiftawi, 191, 192
    (probably same as above).

Abd Allah son of Shelama, 193, 196, 197, 264,
    266, 268, 274, 304.

Ab Hassan of Tyre, 42.

Abischua son of Pinehas, 276, 299.

Abraham al Kabasi, 177, 259, 284.

Abul Al Iz, 188.

Amram, 38, 39, 104, 204, 214, 282, 284, 305,
    306, 307, 308, 365, 366.

Ben Minar, 163, 227.

Eleazar, 118, 173.

Ghazal son of Isaak, 26, 203, 222, 232, 261,
    264, 346.

Huba Allah el Masri, 161, 162, 163, 195.

Hur son of Joseph, 269.

Ibrahim al Jakob al Danfi 23, 24, 29, 114,
    228, 266, 305, 364, 365, 366.

Isaak 182, 252, 254, 268.

Ismail al Rumaihi 230, 259.

Markah, 150, 189, 298, 300.

Matanah the Egyptian, 290.

Murjan, 181, 200, 201, 202, 219, 280, 282.

Musalman al Danfi, 202, 288.

Pinehas son of Eleazar, 182, 268.

Saad Allah, 252, 335.

Other Colophons and Additions. On p. 81 Ragib introduces himself:

(1) מכתב   ראעב
(2) בן   יעקב   בן
(3) ישמעל   בן
(4) אברהם   דמבני
(5) דנפתה   יסלח
(6) לו   יהוה

(1) The writer is Ragib

(2) son of Jakob son of

(3) Ishmael son of

(4) Abraham of the family

(5) Danafite.

(6) Yahweh be merciful to him.

The next colophon is found on p. 216:

(1) הוה . הכלול . מן . אמנות . השלחן . בצפר .

(2) יום . השני . אהד . יום . מן . חדש . רביע .

(3) השני . והוא . חדש . התשיעי . שנת .

(4) אחד . אלף . ושׁשׁה . מאות . ושׁשׁה . שני .

(5) לממלכת . בני . הגר :. / . על . יד . המס ;

(6) הדל . הצריך . לרתות . יהוה . ורחמו ;

(7) ראעב . בן . יעקב . בן . ישמעל :

(8) בן . אברהם . דמבני . דנפתה

(9) יסלח . לו . מרה . דיכל ;

(10) בעמל . משה . הנביותה :

(1)   This completes the provisions of the altar on

(2)   Monday morning the first day of the month of II Rebia

(3)   and it is the ninth month of the year

(4)   1606

(5)   of the reign of the sons of Hagar (A.D. 1889) by the hand of the miserable

(6)   and humble one in need of the awe of Yahweh and his mercy,

(7)   Ragib son of Jakob son of Ishmael

(8)   son of Abraham of the family Danafite.

(9)   Pardon his bitterness of capability;

(10)   By the merit of Moses the prophet.

On p. 234 Ragib writes (in Arabic):

I finished writing this service at
3:15 A.M. on the night of Sunday the 4th
of Jomada II in the year 306 by the poor
one who is asking for the mercy of God
and his forgiveness for the sins he has
committed, the servant of servants,
Ragib, the son of the late Jakob son of
Ishmael son of Ibrahim the Samaritan.
May God forgive him, his sons and all
who taught him. Amen.

The last colophon, also in Arabic, is on p. 346:

This service was finished on Monday
Afternoon the 4th of I Rebia, 1307 A.H.
by the poor one who admits his sins, the
miserable and humble Ragib son of Jakob
son of Ishmael son of Ibrahim the Danafite, the scribe, the Israeli.

There are later museum markings on the inside covers. Inside the front cover, upside
down, is the Three Oaks number 26341 and the
Michigan State University number 2480 CW. On
the facing page the Roman numeral VI is penciled.
Inside the back cover is a penciled "4". On
. 143-44 is a typed note on a card: "Passover
Prayers, Hymns etc. Written by Ragib in 1895."

CW 2486

Passover Prayers
Samaritan with Arabic Instructions
Paper
282 Pages
15.9 x 11.5 cm.
Text: 11.5 x 7.7 cm.
Catchwords

Description. This volume is not as lengthy
nor as richly done (fewer diagrams, changes of
ink color and actual pages) as CW 2480, but it
is similar in content, containing the Service for
the Feast of Passover and the Feast of Unleavened
Bread. It is bound in a red leather cover with
a large arabesque design in the center and similar but smaller designs at each of the four cor-
ners. The first five pages are blank. A poem
is written on the next four pages followed by
three more blank pages, a chart showing the dates
of Passover from A.H. 1306-1401, another blank
page and then the beginning of the first liturgy
on p. 13.

The general text is cursive in black ink on
the same paper as 2480. The "FF PALAZZUOLI"
water mark appears occasionally. For some biblical texts and short liturgical responses majuscule lettering is used. Red and green ink are
sometimes employed for patterns of biblical

verses, instructions and alternative readings.

Designs appear infrequently and a linear dividing line is used on p. 19, 59 and 337. A patch is found on p. 126 with an Arabic note calling upon God to stop the evil in the world. On p. 52 someone has written in dots the word פלגה in the bottom margin. An eight page biblical text in majuscule begins at this point and פלגה may designate this as a "division" between two services. There are extensive scriptural passages in this manuscript, often in triangular patterns of different colors.

A unique feature of this text is the inclusion of a series of secular poems beginning on p. 177. They are all written in Arabic and exalt drinking wine (as in a poem by Ghazal al Rosi, p. 177) sailing at sea, conversations, flowers and maidens (all are part of the poem by the "Moroccan," p. 179ff.). The poems are suggestive of some of the sensuality of the Sufi sect of Islam and Omar Khayyam's *Rubiyat* and add a new dimension to our understanding of the mentality of the Samaritans. Some of them may have sought religious interpretations of the secular symbols by equating God with the wine that one should seek. Others were quite willing to be secular for the moment and, as the note on p. 183 explains: "We are willing to write a few verses of poetry on pleasure which may be said during a time of relaxation and joy."

Scribe and Date. The scribe is Salama son of Amram the Levitical priest. Another copy of the same service by the same scribe written in 1299 (A.D. 1882) is in the British Museum and is described by Cowley as "very cursive and careless" (1909: xiv). Salama is listed in the 1909 census of the Samaritan community (Robertson 1962: 275-76) where we learn that he was born in 1280 (A.D. 1864), had an elder brother Isaak and one daughter, Jamilah, who was 8 years old in 1909. He is listed as a copyist. He was also the scribe of Rylands 41(805), a Samaritan and Hebrew Torah copied in 1899, a text described as "remarkably good" (Robertson 1962: 19). The colophon in that text extends the geneology: Salama son of Amram son of Salamah son of Tabia. He copied a liturgy of Sabbath Services in A.D. 1909 which Dr. Gaster described as "the best copy, written mostly by Shelmah but towards the end a few leaves written by Ishak (his brother), so he told me when selling the manuscript" (Robertson 1962: 69). In 1902 he finished another manuscript, a treatise on the Fatihah by Ibrahim al Qabasi.

Also in the Rylands collection is a letter written presumably to Dr. Gaster by Salama concerning a text of the book of Joshua that the latter had agreed to copy. By this time Salama is high priest of the Samaritan community.

The date of CW 2486 is 1305 (A.D. 1888) at which time the scribe was 24 years old. This is two years earlier than the writing of CW 2480.

Content. The book is divided into nine parts:

I. Service for the first Sabbath of the first month (p. 13ff).

II. Service for the Memorial Sabbath mornings (p. 19ff).

III. Service for the Memorial Sabbath evenings of new moon and exitus (p. 29ff

IV. Service of the second Sabbath of the first month, morning (p. 43ff).

V. Service of Sabbaths of Memorial mornin (p. 59ff).

VI. Instructions for the night of Passover (p. 63ff).

VII. Service for the feast of Passover (p. 79ff).

VIII. Service for the first Sabbath evening

the Seven Days of the Feast of Unleavened Bread (p. 109ff).

IX. Service for the morning of the Seven
Days of the Feast of Unleavened Bread
(p. 129ff).

Hymn Writers. The hymn writers cited by
name in this volume are:

Abdullah son of Salama, 61.

Abischua son of Pinehas, 205.

Abraham son of Jakob, 44, 252.

Amram, 140, 271.

Eleazar, 183, 193.

Fatarhi, 184, 186.

Ghazal, 15, 164, 209, 248.

Ghazal al Maturri, 165, 177.

Ibrahim al Danfi, 132, 135, 139, 171, 202.

Ibrahim Kabasi, 195, 196, 198.

Markah, 156, 191, 192, 272.

Murtaj Rasi son of Chedar son of Isaak, 6,
148.

Pinehas the Levite, 274.

Saad son of Saadun, 163.

Tabia son of Joseph son of Abraham, 247.

Other Colophons and Additions. At the top
of p. 203 this note appears in Arabic:

I finished writing this book of
services on the 13th of I Jomada, 1305
(A.D. 1888), the servant of God, Salama
son of Amram, the Levite priest. God
forgive him and place his soul in
Paradise.

In the middle of the page a second note appears:

I gave this book to my brother
Ismail son of Safi son of Isaak the
Danafite. May God repay me and bless
it and his descendents and may his

descendents and their descendents learn
from it. Amen. Amen. 16th of the 11th
month 1307 (A.D. 1890), Salama the
priest.

One other note appears at the bottom of the page:

I gave this book to my brother
Abdul Mulugub--Abdel who is nicknamed
Shamon--son of Jakob Sarawi the Danafite.
May God compensate him and make it a
blessing on his descendents and may his
grandchildren and great grandchildren
make use of it. Amen. Amen. 28th Ragab
1310 (A.D. 1893), Ismail Sali Sephar the
Danafite.

Ismail, to whom the scribe gave the book according to the second note, may be the Ishmael
son of Shelah listed in the census list as 48
years old and the מבחר of the Samaritan community. The second recipient is otherwise unknown.

A penciled "II" appears at the top inside of
the front cover. In the middle of the page are
written the following Arabic numerals:

76	2
98	5
175	7

CW 10312

Day of Atonement
Samaritan with Arabic Instructions
Paper
190 Pp. 22 x 12 cm.
Text: 15 x 9.3 cm.
Catchwords

Description. This manuscript contains the services for the Day of Atonement "following the special ·tradition of the great Hakbor," according to an Arabic note found on the second page and dated the 28th of Zophar 1284 (A.D. 1863). It is written in black ink, with occasional use of a contrasting red, on cheaper paper than the previous two manuscripts, but with a similar tooled red leather cover. A water mark in Arabic appears in the lower right hand corner of p. 162.

Throughout the manuscript there is a system of Arabic numbering. It presumably counts the lines, but the numbers are not always in order and their function is not clear. The text itself is in a minuscule hand similar to the previous two liturgies.

In a poem on pp. 87-88 there are 28 lines beginning with the word קל and both ends of the lines are bordered by a four dot design. Similar patterns of four dots are found on pp. 92-95, enclosing a poem with a complex acrostic structure. A poem by Murjan al Danfi is enclosed in a marginal design on pp. 153-54. The pattern uses the four dots and also a series of check-like marks. On p. 166 a poem by Nanak is bracketed.

Scribe and Date. The main colophon reads (in Arabic):

This book of worship was finished with the help of God on Thursday night at the time of the Ishat prayers the 25th of 1st Rebia (5th month) 1284 (A.D. 1863) by the servant of God who has submitted completely to God and admitted his sins, Ishmael son of Israeli son of Ishmael son of Ibrahim al Danfi, writer of Aktar. May God forgive him and his ancestors and his descendents. Amen. Amen.

Presumably it is Ishmael's death that is recorded in 1866 on the fly leaf of a Service for the Dead in the Rylands collection (Robertson 1962:77). He appears as witness in a dispute over the ownership of another manuscript in the year of his death (Robertson 1962: 83) and as one of the poets in a treatise written in 1899 (Robertson 1962: 126).

Content. There is only one title in the work:

צלות . יום .הכפור . העום . הו .:

Service for the Day of Atonement.
How Great it is!

Hymn Writers.

Abdullah son of Salama, 19, *129*, 130, *229*.
Abisschua, 178.
Absichua son of Pinehas, 27, 53.
Ab . . . Koh son of Abraham, 114.
Abraham Kabasi, 84, *90*, *145*, *163*, *190*, *229*, *245*, *263*.
Abu-Asarim Sufi il-iz son of al Matari, *149*, *249*.
Al Ahmad Ismail al Ruhmeihi, Murjan al Danfi, 181, *281*.
Amram, 11, *132*, *232*.
Areas Mitshah al Mudat, 285.
Ben Minar, 22, 262.
Ghazal, 6, 115, 120, 141, 220, 237, 240.
Hasan al Suri, 6.
Ibrahim son of Jakob son of Murjan al Danfi, 6, 115, *122*, *222*.
Israel, 276.
Joseph, 91.
Markah, 99, 124.
Morin son of Sadaqa Hafnawi, 277.
Mufaraj Jakob Mufaraj, *114*, *166*, *266*.
Murjan, *152*, *252*, 253, 281.

Musalam, 114.
Muslim al Murjan, 66.
Nanak son of Markah, 166.
Pinehas son of Joseph, 125.
Pinehas son of Othmar, *148, 248.*
Saada son of Kathar *160, 260.*

Of special note in this listing is the number of times that two poems by the same hymn writer are exactly 100 pp. apart. The instances italicized above seem too frequent for chance.

Other Colophons and Additions. On the same page as the first colophon is a second, also in Arabic:

This Holy Book is given to the foreigner, Mr. Whiting; may he compensate me, nevertheless, it becomes a part of his own personal property, 5th (month) 1332 (A.D. 1914).

On the inside of the front cover is a penciled "5" and in Arabic, "160 Gurush." On the back inside cover is written:

26345
10312 CW
5

CW 10313

Passover Prayers
Samaritan with Arabic Instructions
Paper
162 Pp.
21.5 cm. x 15.8 cm.
Text: 14.8 cm. x 10.2 cm.
Catchwords

Description. The book is bound in black and white spotted cardboard and red leather. There are two watermarks on the paper: "London-eone" and "Carurera de Mori," both written in a flowing script. Most of the writing is in black ink, but green and red inks were also used. The cursive writing is generally quite good except for the final pages which seem to have been done hastily. An obvious change of hands occurs on p. 26 where the ink becomes more intense and the size of the letters is smaller. That hand continues for the rest of the book.

Corrections were made by Kadir Isaak. On p. 37 is a note explaining that certain hymns had been forgotten and were written in by Kadir. He also makes an addition on p. 64. His identity is otherwise unknown. Special care is given to a series of responses on pp. 54-56. The responses are in separate columns in alternating black and red and the lines are bracketed in the margins with a series of three backward commas.

Scribe and Date. The most important colophon is in Arabic and reads:

Finished on Friday the 16th of Muhurram 1332 by Barhum Sarawi. God forgive him. The owner of this comforting book is Chebab ibn Shamoun al Marhum Abdel Atif Sarawi. God forgive him all his sins. Amen.

The owner is not otherwise known. The scribe is cited in other manuscripts. Barhum is an alternate or pet name of Abraham (Robertson 1962: 155). There is an Abram son of Joseph in the 1909 census list who was a 32 year old clothier. He had a brother two years younger who was a servant to a gentile. He is the scribe of a treatise "Sepher Hilluk" written in 1920 (Robertson 1962: 145-46) and a set of seven treatises written in 1330 (A.D. 1911) (Robertson 1962: 155-57) in which he is identified as Barhum son of Joseph son of Abdul Latif, al Sarawi.

He copied 10313 in 1322 (A.D. 1904) when he would have been 27 years old.

Content. It consists of the following parts:

I. Service for Samut Passover, the first sabbath (p. 1).

II. Usual noon Prayer (p. 31).

III. Service for the evening of the first month (p. 39).

IV. Service for the morning of the day of the day of the first month (p. 75).

V. Service for the day of the first month when it is a Sabbath. (p. 103).

Hymn Writers.

Abdullah Salama, 24, 115, 154.
Ben Minar, 3.
Ghazal, 120, 219, 154.
Isaak son of Amram, 31.
Isaak son of Musalama, 27.
Joseph, 126.
Markah, 45.
Matanah, the Egyptian, 26.
Murjan al Danfi, 112, 128.
Pinehas, 93.

Other Colophons and Additions. A second colophon, also in Arabic, reads:

This comforting piece was given to Mr. Warren Whiting. He is from the American Committee in Jerusalem and he compensated him by some arrangement. The first day of the 5th month, I Jomada 1332 (A.D. 1909), Helmi.

The only Helmi listed in the 1909 census is Hilmi son of Jakob, a 29 year old father of a 4 year old son. He has three brothers, only one of whom is listed as having an occupation. He is of the Danafite family.

Only the catalogue numbers appear on both front and back inside covers. 26346; CW 10313.

CW 26343

Parts of the Defter
Samaritan with Arabic Instructions
Paper
280 pp.
10 x 15 cm.
Text: 15.2 x 7.8 cm.
Catchwords

Description. This volume seems to be a composite of various parts of the Defter or basic prayer book of the Samaritans. It has a brown leather cover over which green cloth has been glued. There are obviously some pages missing both at the end and within the text.

On pp. 1-2 is a chart equating the Arabic and Syrian calendar. Pp. 4, 5 and 6 are all badly discolored and more than half of the page in each case is covered with a patch. Other patches appear on pp. 18, 23, 55, 70 and 80. One or more pages are missing beginning at pp. 38, 60, 94 and 280. A different hand has done pp. 10-11 and several different handwritings are discernible after p. 259.

Scribe and Date. The major colophon is probably lost with the last pages of the book, but other colophons identify the scribe as Murjan son of Ibrahim son of Ismail al Danfi. He is the scribe of many of the works listed in Cowley and Robertson. 26343 was finished in 1136 (A.D. 1724), which makes it the oldest of the liturgical manuscripts in the Chamberlain-Warren collec-

collection.

Content. The volume is a collection of liturgical pieces, chiefly *manats* and other hymns
to be used on various sabbaths, the unrolling of
the scroll, Passover, Seventh Month, Yom Kippur
and Season of Pilgrimmage.

Hymn Writers.

Abdul Hassan, 209, 225, 226.

Abu Hasan al Khouri, 53.

Al Dustan, 208, 224, 225.

Amram, 64.

Eleazar, 163, 177.

Joseph, 233.

Markah, 32, 37, 48, 131, 136, 140, 177, 196,
  210, 213, 227.

Mufaraj, 231.

Murjan son of Ibrahim, 207, 225, 229, 234.

Muslim, 226.

Nanah son of Markah, 53.

Pinehas, 89, 172, 182, 196, 228, 230.

Said al Issa, 221.

Other Colophons and Additions. Four similar
notes mark the completion of various parts of the
text, each bearing the date 1136 (A.D. 1724).
The one on p. 80, for example, reads:

> Finished this Durran Monday morning
> 23rd of Ramazan 1136 (A.D. 1724) by Mur-
> jan ibn Ibrahim ibn Ismail al Danfi.
> God forgive him and forgive his father
> and all the inhabitants of Mt. Gerizim.

The last colophon reads:

> We finished two copies (another
> like this) on Wednesday morning the
> 15th of Shawwal 1136 (A.D. 1724) and

these prayers from the sayings of
Mufaraj al Mufaraj.

The inside cover bears the number 5 and the
Three Oaks catalogue number 26343. This volume,
like some of the others does not contain a CW
number. The inside back cover is quite wrinkled
and bears penciled columns in which nothing was
written.

CW 26344

Festival of Booths
Samaritan with Arabic Instructions
Paper
147 Pp.
16.3 x 20 cm.
Text: 15.5 x 11 cm.
Catchwords

Description. This book consists primarily
of *manats* and other hymns associated with the
Festival of Booths. It is contained in a tooled
brown leather cover to which a paper design has
been pasted. Most of it was written in black
ink with occasional use of red. It is somewhat
more carelessly written than the other texts in
this collection.

Major divisions are marked off by horizontal
red and black zigzag lines on p. 46, groups of 3
backward 7's on p. 68 and a single horizontal
zigzag line on pp. 12 and 93. Pp. 47-56 are
blank.

Scribe and Date. The last colophon simply
states, in Arabic, "Finished by Joseph son of
Israeli." A fuller reading of his name is Joseph
son of Israel son of Ishmael son of Abraham as
Sarawi al Danfi. Another of his works is Codex
XII of the Rylands collection completed in the
same year (A.H. 1277/A.D. 1860). He is also

listed as having consulted a treatise on dogma by Sadaqa al Israeli in II Ragib of the same year.

Content.

I.   Prayers for the ten days of הסליהות,
    evening (p. 2).
II. Service for the night of the seven days
    of the Festival of Booths (p. 57).
III. Service of the days of the seven days
    of the Festival of Booths, morning
    (p. 69).
IV. Service of the last Sabbath of the
    Festival of Booths (p. 97).

Hymns/Writers.

Abraham, 101.
Abu Izzi Katari, 121.
Amram, 146.
Eleazar, 122, 140.
Hiba Tula El Masra, 143.
Markah, 72, 91.
Murjan, 112.
Pinehas, 105.
Saadin al Kafari, 100, 105.

Other Colophons and Additions. There are several colophons in the book:

P. 2:   We started writing this the 10th of 1
    Rebia 1277 (A.D. 1860).
P. 10: By his slave Joseph El Israeli, Mond
    1st Rebia 1277 (A.D. 1860).
P. 14: This prayer took only two hours.
P. 44: Finished Monday morning the 15th of
    Rebia by Joseph son of Israel as Sarawi as
    Samar.
P. 68: Finished Thursday morning II Rebia b
    Joseph Israel 1277 (A.D. 1860).
P. 93: We finished writing these prayers of
    Seven Days on Friday afternoon the 6th of
    II Rebia which is the 10th month of 1277
    (A.D. 1860) corresponding to the 7th of II
    Tishri 1276 of the Roman (?) calendar by t
    writer Joseph son of Isreal son of Ismail
    son of Ibrahim who is the writer of al Mer
    and Mr. Ismael Halaby helped me a great de
    in this hard work. God forgive him and ma
    our descendents make use of it.
P. 152: Finished by Joseph son of Israel.
P. 152: Given to Mr. Warren Whiting. He is
    a member of the American Committee in
Jerusalem. 1332 (A.D. 1909) according to the
Roman calendar.

FIGURES

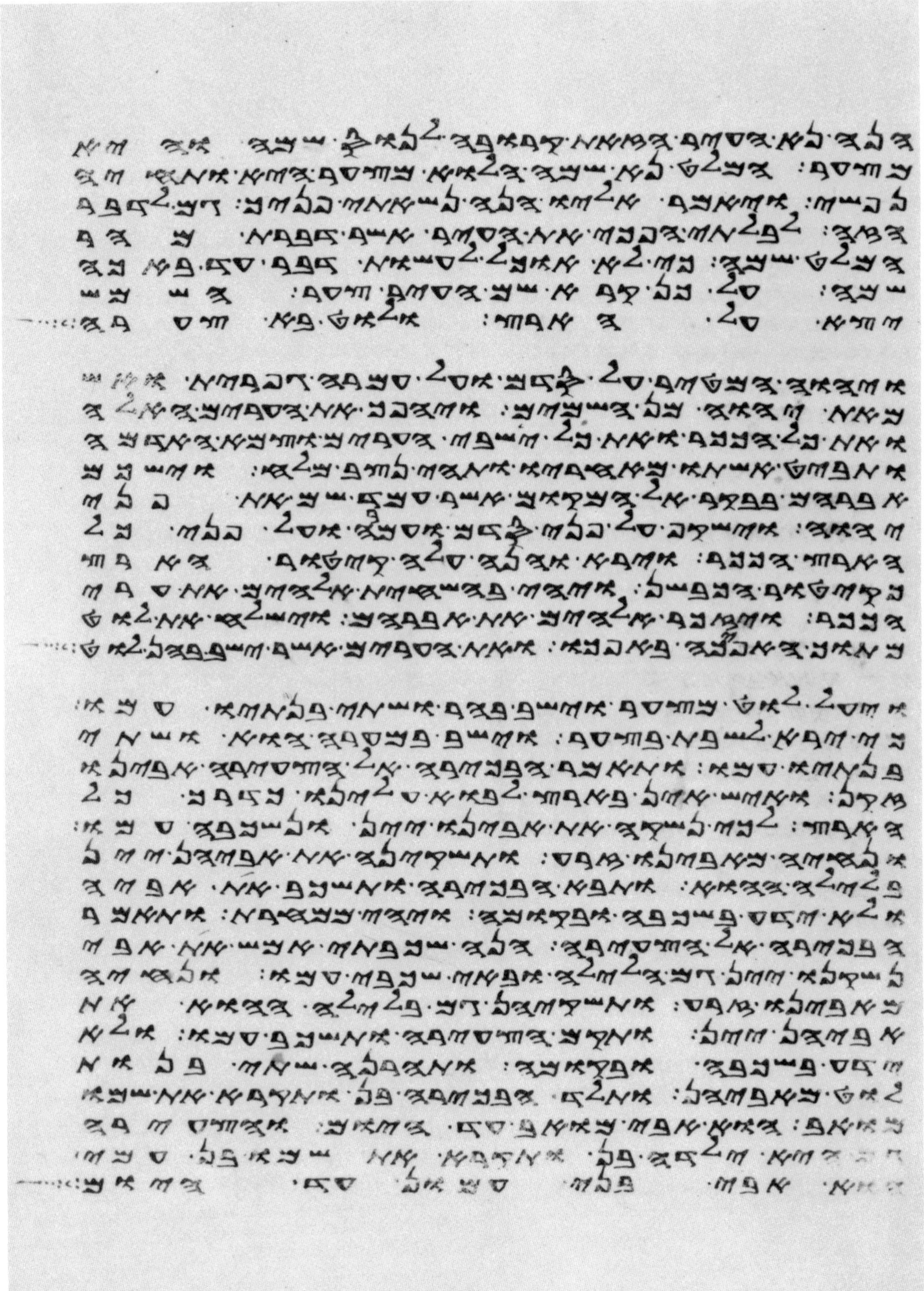

Fig. 1

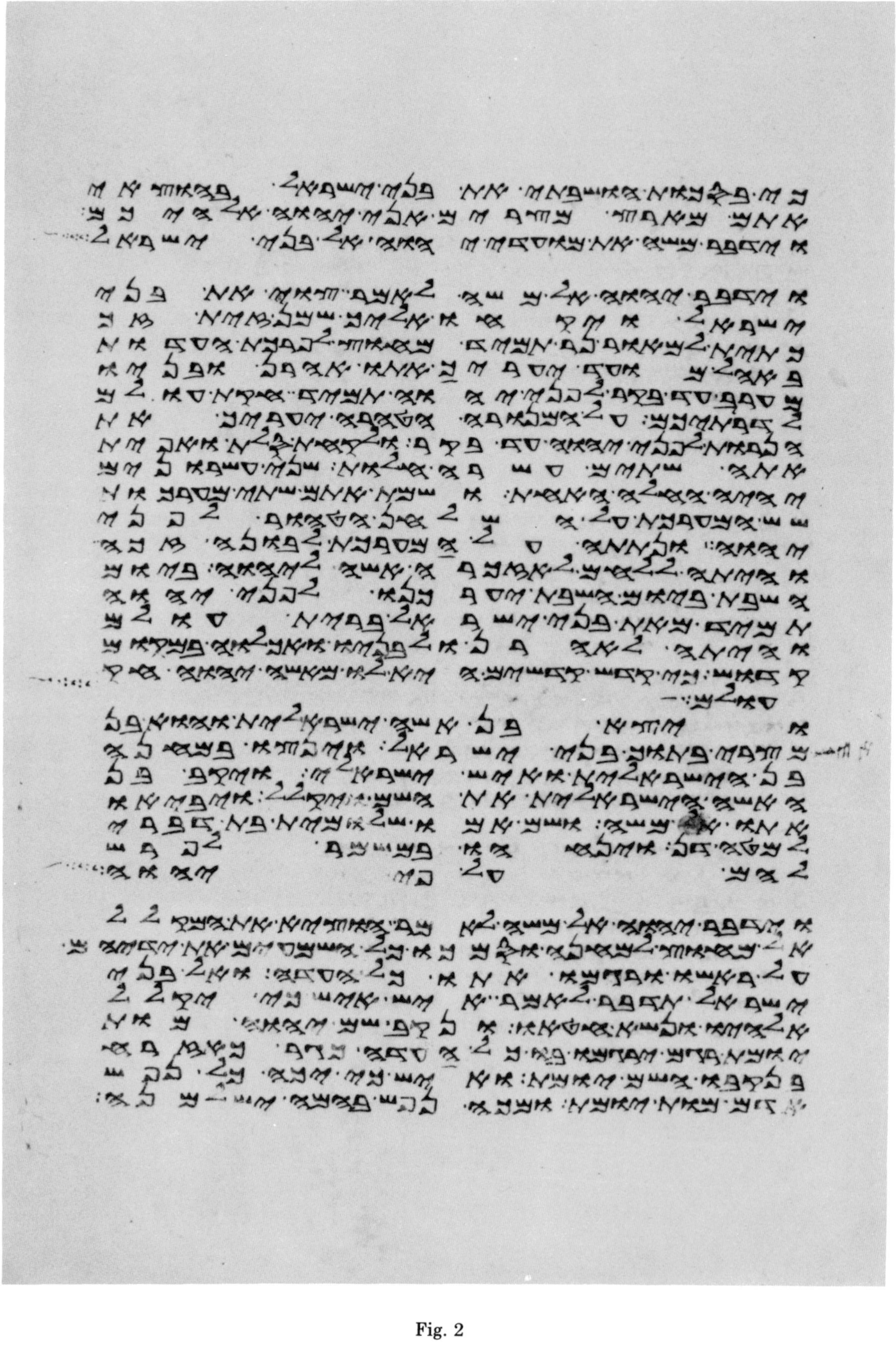

Fig. 2

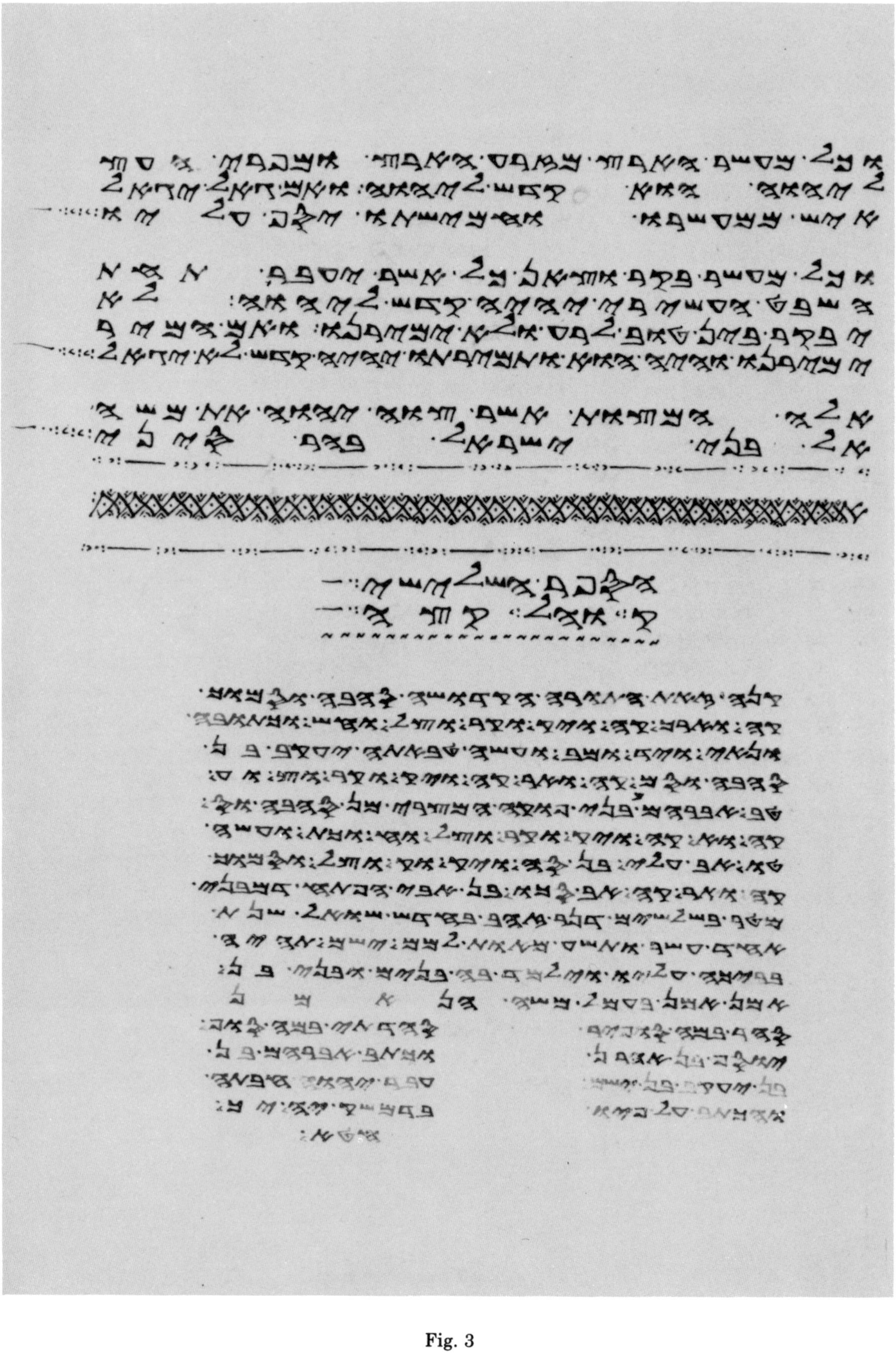

Fig. 3

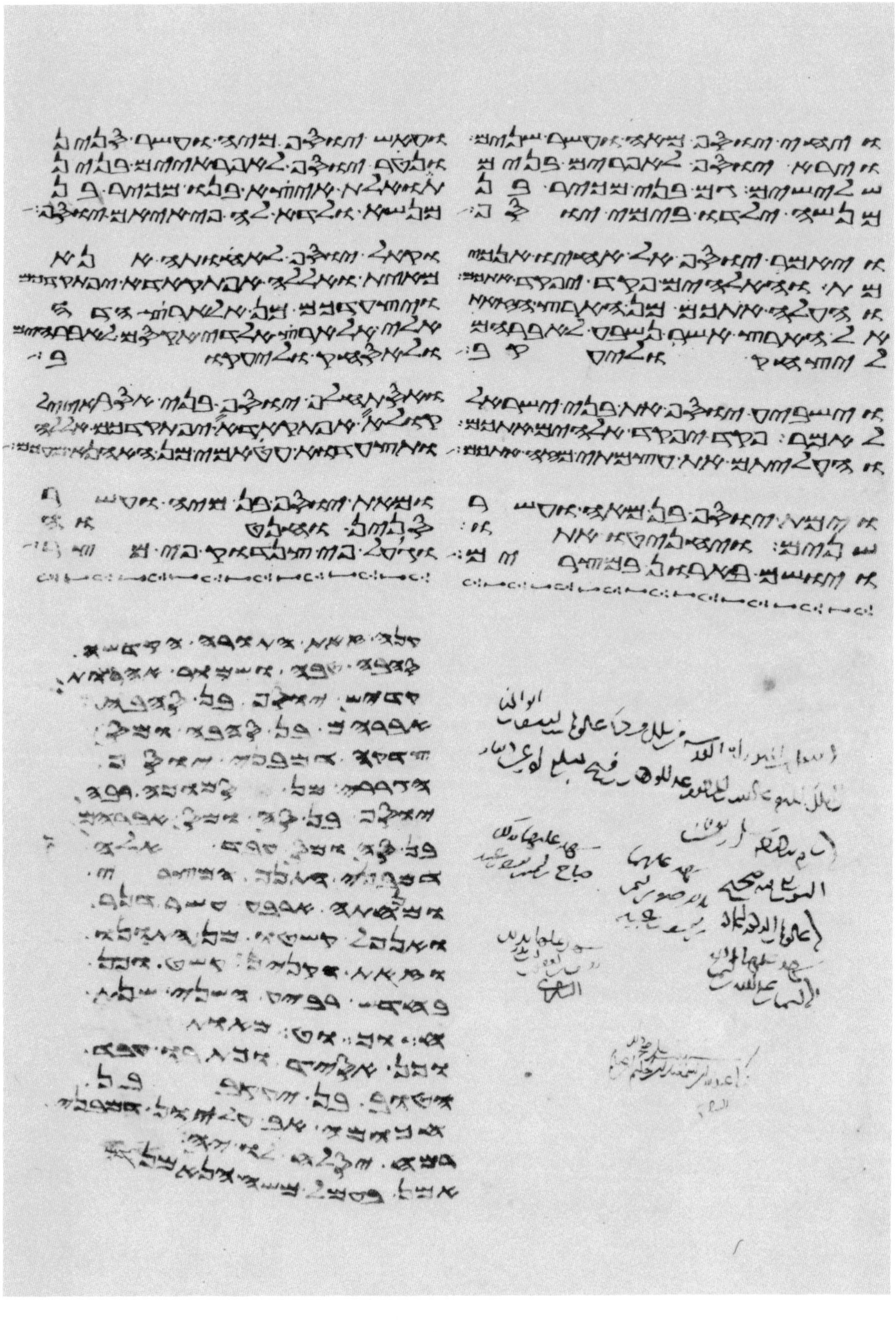

Fig. 4

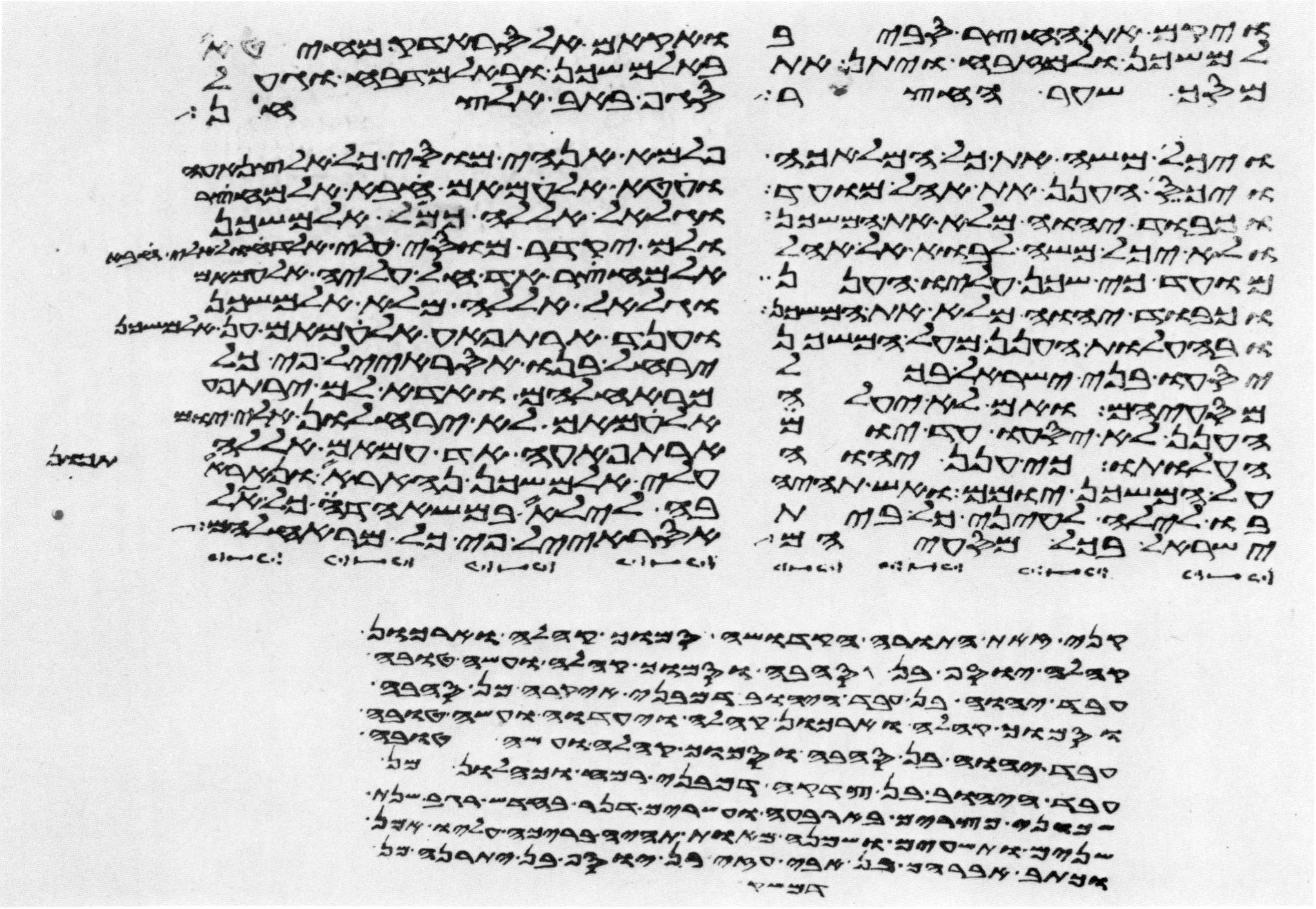

Fig. 5

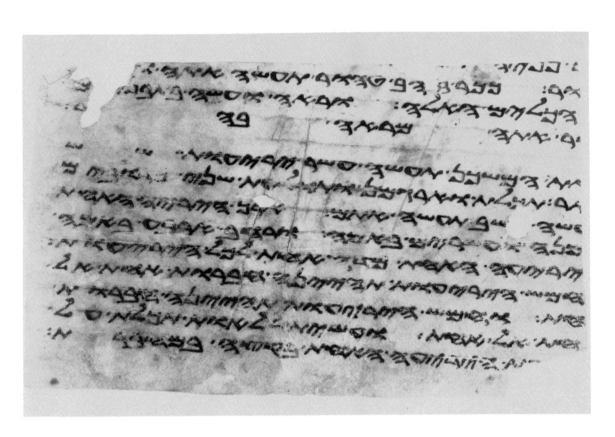

Fig. 6

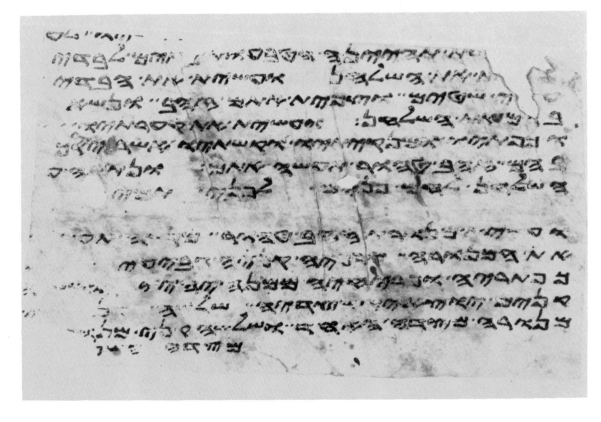

Fig. 7

Fig. 8

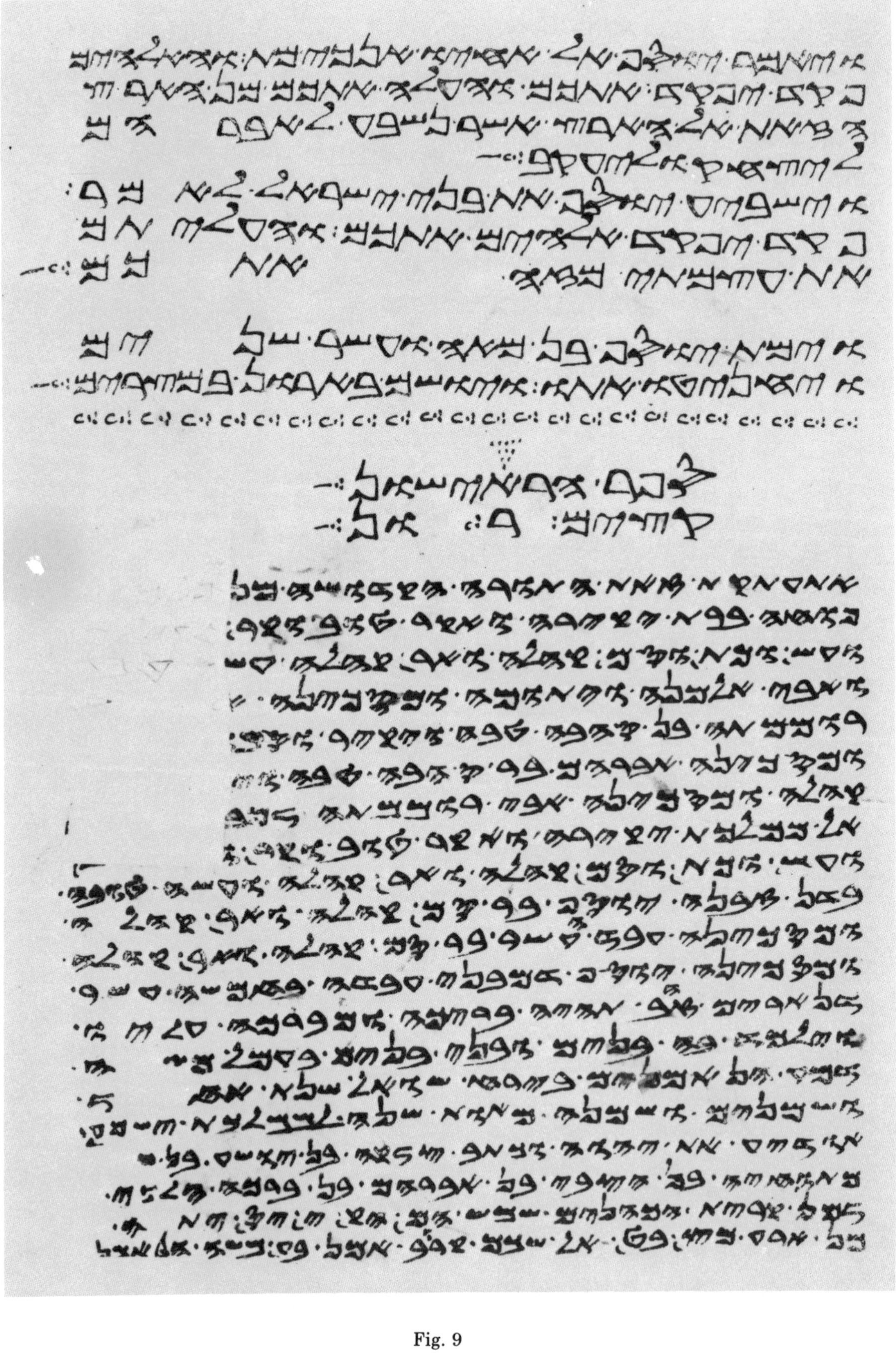

Fig. 9

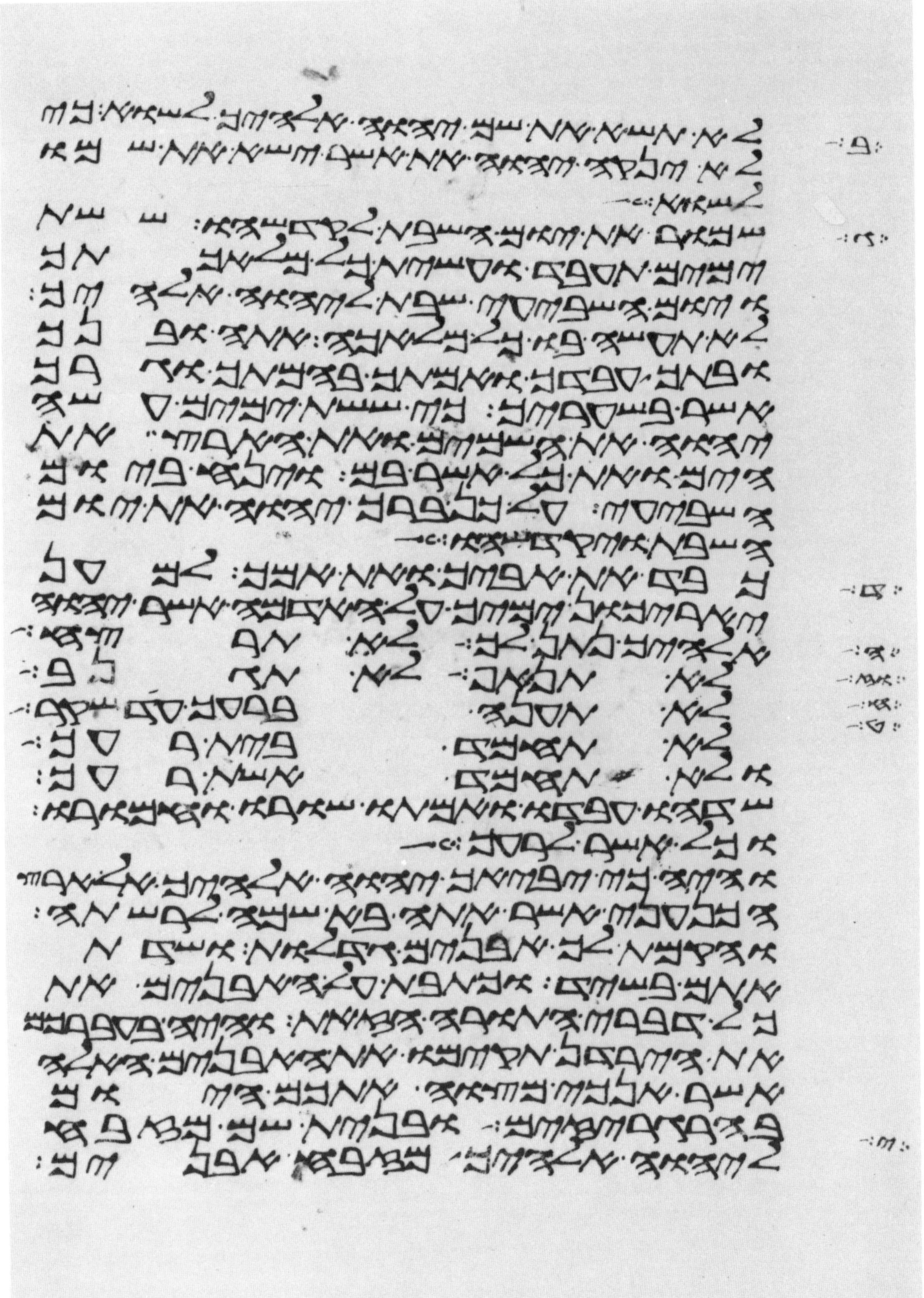

Fig. 10

Fig. 11

Fig. 12

BIBLIOGRAPHY

Abel, F. M.

1906   Inscription samaritaine de Gaza et in-
       scriptions grecques de Bersabee.
       Revue biblique 15: 84-87.

Adler, E. K., and Seligsohn, M.

1902a Une nouvelle chronique samaritaine.
       Revue des etudes Juives 44: 188-222.

1902b Une nouvelle chronique samaritaine.
       Revue des etudes Juives 45: 70-98,
       160, 223-54.

1903   Une nouvelle chronique samaritaine.
       Revue des etudes Juives 46: 123-46.

Alt, A.

1925   Zwei samaritanische Inschriften.
       *Zeitschrift des deutschen Palästina-
       Vereins* 48: 398-400.

1952   Zu den samaritanischen Dekalogin-
       schriften. *Vetus Testamentum* 2:
       237-76.

Anderson, R. T.

1970   Le Pentateuque samaritaine Chamber-
       lain-Warren CW 2473. *Revue biblique*
       77: 68-75.

1970a Le Pentateuque samaritaine Chamber-
       lain-Warren CW 2478A. *Revue biblique*
       77: 550-60.

1972   Le Pentateuque samaritaine Chamber-
       lain-Warren CW 2484. *Revue biblique*
       79: 368-80.

Baillet, M.

1960   Un nouveau fragment du pentateuque
       samaritaine. *Revue biblique* 67:
       49-57.

Barton, W. E.

1921   The War and the Samaritan Colony.
       Bibliotheca Sacra 78: 1-22.

Ben-Zvi, Y.

1930   A Samaritan Inscription from Kaft
       Quallil. *Journal of the Palestine
       Oriental Society* 10: 222-26.

1941   The Beit el-Mā Samaritan Inscription.
       *Bulletin of the American Schools of
       Oriental Research* 84: 2-4.

1942a Migginze Shomron. *Sinai* 10: 100-06,
       215-22.

1942b Migginze Shomron. *Sinai* 11: 156-62

1943a Migginze Shomron. *Sinai* 12: 410-17

1943b Migginze Shomron. *Sinai* 13: 245-51,
       308-18.

1943c Migginze Shomron. *Sinai* 14: 17-20.

1961   A Lamp with a Samaritan Inscription:
       There is None Like unto Thee, O God
       of Jeshurun. *Israel Exploration
       Journal* 11: 139-42.

Bowman, J.

1950-51 Samaritan Decalogue Inscriptions.
       Bulletin of the John Rylands Library
       33: 211-36.

1951   The Leeds Samaritan Decalogue Inscrip-
       tion. *Proceedings of the Leeds
       Philosophical Society* 1: 567-75.

1957-58 The Samaritans and the Book of Deuter-
       onomy. *Transactions of the Glasgow
       University Oriental Society* 17: 9-18.

1958   Samaritan Studies. *Bulletin of the
       John Rylands Library* 40: 298-327.

1967   *Samaritanische Probleme. Studien zum*
        Verhältnis von Samaritanertum,
        Judentum und Urchristentum. Stutt-
        gart: Kohlhammer.

Campbell, E. F.

1969   Hadrianic and Samaritan Temples. *ASOR*
        Newsletter 10: 5-8.

Castro, P.

1953   El Sefer Abisha. *Sefarad* 13: 119-29.

Clermont-Ganneau, C.

1882   Expedition to Amwas (Emmaus-Nicopolis).
        Palestine Exploration Fund Quarterly
        Statement: 22-37.

1904   Une nouvelle chronique samaritaine.
        Journal des savants 2: 34.

1906   Inscription samaritaine de Gaza et
        inscriptions grecques de Bersebee.
        Revue biblique 15: 87-91.

1966   Aspects of Samaritan and Jewish His-
        tory in Late Persian and Hellenistic
        Times. *Harvard Theological Review*
        59: 201-11.

Coggins, R. J.

1968   The Old Testament and Samaritan Ori-
        gins. *Annual of the Swedish Theolog-*
        ical Institute 6: 35-48.

1975   *Samaritans and Jews: The Origins of*
        Samaritanism Reconsidered. Atlanta:
        John Knox.

Condor, C. R.

1885   The Samaritan Temple. *Quarterly*
        Statement of the Palestine Explora-
        tion Fund: 19.

1904   Description of Four Samaritan Manu-
        scripts belonging to the Palestine
        Exploration Fund. *Quarterly State-*
        ment of the Palestine Exploration
        Fund: 67-68.

1904b   A Supposed Early Copy of the Samaritan
        Pentateuch. *Quarterly Statement of*
        the Palestine Exploration Fund:
        394-96.

Cowley, A.

1905   Samaritans. Pp. 669-81 in Vol. 10 o[
        The Jewish Encyclopedia, ed. I.
        Singer. New York: Funk and Wagnalls

1909   *The Samaritan Liturgy.* 2 Vols.
        Oxford: Oxford University.

Gall, A. von

1914-18 *Der Hebräische Pentateuch der Samari*
        taner. Reprint 1966. Giessen:
        Topelmann.

Gaster, M.

1900   A Samaritan Scroll of the Hebrew
        Pentateuch. *Proceedings of the Soci*
        ety of Biblical Archaeology 22:
        240-69.

1909   The Chain of Samaritan High Priests.
        Journal of the Royal Asiatic Society
        393-420.

1925   *The Samaritans, Their History, Doc-*
        trines, and Literature. London:
        Oxford University.

1925-28 *Studies and Texts in Folklore, Magic*
        Medieval Romance, Hebrew Apocrypha
        and Samaritan Archaeology. 3 Vols.
        London: Maggs.

Gottheil, R.

1906   The Dating of their Manuscripts by t[
        Samaritans. *Journal of Biblical*
        Literature 25: 29-48.

Halkin, A. S.

1935-36 Samaritan Polemics against the Jews.
        Proceedings of the American Academy
        of Jewish Research 7: 13-59.

Haran, M.

1974   The Song of the Precepts of Aaron be[
        Manir. *Proceedings of the Israel*
        Academy of Sciences and Humanities
        5: 174-209.

Harkavy, A. E.

1866   *Catalogue des manuscrits hebreux et*
        samaritains de la biblioteque
        imperiale. Paris.

1874   The Collection of Samaritan Manu-
        scripts at St. Petersburg. Appendix
        I in *Fragments of a Samaritan Targum*,
        by J. W. Nutt. London: Trubner.

Kahle, P.
1953   The Abisha[c] Scroll of the Samaritans.
        Pp. 188-92 in *Studia Orientalia Ioanni*
        Pedersen. Hauniae: Munksgaard.

Kippenberg, H. G.
1971   Gerizim und Synagoge: Traditions-
        geschichtliche Untersuchungen zur
        samaritanischen Religion der aramäis-
        chen Periode. *Religionsgeschichtliche*
        Versuche und Vorarbeiten 30: Berlin:
        De Gruyter.

Lagrange, M. J.
1890   Decouverte d'une inscription en carac-
        teres samaritains a Amouas. *Terre*
        Sainte: 339.

1891   L'inscription samaritaine d'Amwas.
        Terre Sainte: 83-84.

1893a   Inscription samaritaine d'Amwas.
        Revue biblique 2: 114.

1893b   Inscription samaritaine d'Amwas.
        Revue biblique 2: 433-34.

MacDonald, J.
1960   The Samaritain Doctrine of Moses.
        Scottish Journal of Theology 13:
        149-62.

1963   *Memar Marqah*. 2 Vols. *Beihefte zur*
        Zeitschrift für die alttestamentliche
        Wissenschaft 84. Berlin: Topelmann.

1964   *The Theology of the Samaritans*.
        London: SCM.

Mayer, L. A.
1964   *Bibliography of the Samaritans*. Sup-
        plements to Abr-Nahrain 1, ed. D.
        Broadribb. Leiden: Brill.

Montgomery, J. A.
1907   *The Samaritans, the Earliest Jewish*
        Sects. Their History, Theology and
        Literature. Philadelphia: Winston.

        Reprint 1968. New York: KTAV.

Moore, G. F.
1888   On a Fragment of a Samaritan Penta-
        teuch in the Library of the Andover
        Theological Seminary. *Journal of the*
        American Oriental Society 14: xxxv.

Moulton, W. J.
1904   The Samaritan Passover. *Journal of*
        Biblical Religion 22: 187-94.

Payne Smith, R.
1863   The Samaritan Chronicle of Abul Fatah,
        the Arabic Text from the Manuscript in
        the Bodleian Library with a Literal
        English Translation. Pp. 304, 432 in
        Vierteljahrschrift fur deutsch-
        englisch-theologische Forschung und
        Kritik, ed. M. Heidenheim.

Perez Castro, F.
1959   *Sefer Abisa[c], Edicion del Fragmento*
        antiguo del Rollo sagrado Pentateuco
        hebreo samaritano de Nablus: Estudio,
        Transcripcion, Aparato critico y
        Facsimiles. Textos y Estudios del
        Seminario Fililogico Cardenal Cis-
        neros. Madrid: C. S. I. C.

Plumptre, E. H.
1878   The Samaritan Element in the Gospel
        and Acts. *The Expositer* 7: 22-40.

Pritchard, W. I.
1873   Note on the Newly Discovered Samari-
        tan Stone. *Palestine Exploration*
        Fund, Quarterly Statement: 118.

Purvis, J. D.
1965   Ben Sira and the Foolish People of
        Shechem. *Journal of Near Eastern*
        Studies 24: 88-94.

1968   *The Samaritan Pentateuch and the*
        Origin of the Samaritan Sect.
        Cambridge: Harvard University.

1972   Studies on Samaritan Materials in the
        W. E. Barton Collection in the Boston
        Library. Pp. 134-43 in *Actes du V*[e]

congres international des etudes Juives. Jerusalem: World Union of Jewish Studies.

Robertson, E.

1937   Notes and Extracts from the Semitic Manuscripts in the John Rylands Library. *Bulletin of the John Rylands Library* 21: 244-72.

1938   *Catalogue of the Samaritan Manuscripts in the John Rylands Library, Manchester I.* Manchester: John Rylands Library.

1962   *Catalogue of the Samaritan Manuscripts in the John Rylands Library, Manchester II.* Manchester: John Rylands Library.

Rosen, G.

1860   Über samaritanische Inschriften. *Zeitschrift der Deutschen Morgenländischen Gesellschaft* 15: 622-31.

Rowley, H. H.

1955   Sanballat and the Samaritan Temple. *Bulletin of the John Rylands Library* 38: 166-98.

1962   The Samaritan Schism in Legend and History. Pp. 208-22 in *Israel's Prophetic Heritage: Essays in Honor of James Muilenberg,* ed. B. W. Anderson and W. Harrelson. New York: Harper.

Sassoon, D. S.

1932   *Descriptive Catalogue of the Hebrew and Samaritan Manuscripts in the Sassoon Library.* London: Oxford University.

Shunnar, Z.

1974   *Katalog Samaritanischer Handinschriften I.* Berlin-West: Seitz.

Skehen, P. W.

1955   Exodus in the Samaritan Recension from Qumran. *Journal of Biblical Studies* 74: 182-87.

Spiro, A.

1951   Samaritans, Tobiads, and Judahites in Pseudo-Philo. *Proceedings of the Academy of Jewish Research* 20: 279-355.

Spoer, H.

1906   The Description of the Case of the Roll of a Samaritan Pentateuch. *Journal of the American Oriental Society* 27: 105-7.

1908   Notes on Some New Samaritan Inscriptions. *Proceedings of the Society of Biblical Archaeology* 30: 284-91.

Strugnell, J.

1967   Quelques inscriptions samaritaines. *Revue biblique* 74: 555-80.

Taylor, W. R.

1930   Recent Epigraphic Discoveries in Palestine. *Journal of the Palestine Oriental Society* 10: 16-22.

1936   A Samaritan Inscription from Gaza. *Journal of the Palestine Oriental Society* 16: 131-37.

1941   A New Samaritan Inscription. *Bulletin of the American Schools of Oriental Research* 81: 1-6.

Trotter, R. J. F.

1961   Did the Samaritans of the Fourth Century Know the Epistle to the Hebrews? *Leeds University Oriental Society, Monograph Series* 1.

Vogue, M. de

1896   Nouvelle inscription d'Amwas. *Revue biblique* 5: 433-34.

Waltke, B. K.

1965   *Prolegomena to the Samaritan Pentateuch.* Unpublished Ph.D. dissertation. Cambridge: Harvard University.

Wright, G. E.

1962   The Samaritans at Shechem. *Harvard Theological Review* 55: 357-66.

Yonick, S.

    1967   The Samaritan Inscription from Siyagha: A Reconstruction and Restudy. Pp. 162–221 in *Studii Biblici Franciscani, Liber Annus* 17. Jerusalem: Aedum Flagellationis.